The PowerX Strategy

How to Trade Stocks and Options in Only 15 Minutes a Day

Second Edition

By Markus Heitkoetter

Information within this publication contains "forward looking statements" within the meaning of Section 27A of the Securities Act of 1933 and Section 21B of the Securities Exchange Act of 1934. Any statements that express or involve discussions with respect to predictions, goals, expectations, beliefs, plans, projections, objectives, assumptions or future events or performance are not statements of historical fact and may be "forward looking statements." Forward looking statements are based on expectations, estimates and projections at the time the statements are made that involve a number of risks and uncertainties which could cause actual results or events to differ materially from those presently anticipated. Investing involves the risk of loss as well as the possibility of profit. All investments involve risk, and all investment decisions of an individual remain the responsibility of that individual. Option and stock investing involves risk and is not suitable for all investors. Past performance does not guarantee future results. No statement in this book should be construed as a recommendation to buy or sell a security. The author and publisher of this book cannot guarantee that the strategies outlined in this book will be profitable and will not be held liable for any possible trading losses related to these strategies.

All information provided within this publication pertaining to investing, options, stocks and securities is educational information and not investment advice. Rockwell Trading is not an investment advisor and recommends all readers and subscribers to seek advice from a registered professional securities representative before deciding to invest in stocks and options featured within this publication. None of the material within this publication shall be construed as any kind of investment advice. Readers of this publication are cautioned not to place undue reliance on forward looking statements, which are based on certain assumptions and expectations involving various risks and uncertainties that could cause results to differ materially from those set forth in the forward looking statements. Please be advised that nothing within this publication shall constitute a solicitation or an invitation to buy or sell any security mentioned herein. The author of this publication is neither a registered investment advisor nor affiliated with any broker or dealer.

Although every precaution has been taken in the preparation of this publication, the publisher and author assume no liability for errors and omissions. This publication is published without warranty of any kind, either expressed or implied. Furthermore, neither the author nor the publisher shall be liable for any damages, either directly or indirectly arising from the use or misuse of the book. Users of this publication agree to indemnify, release and hold harmless Rockwell Trading, its members, employees, agents, representatives, affiliates, subsidiaries, successors and assigns (collectively, "The Companies") from and against any and all claims, liabilities, losses, causes of actions, costs, lost profits, lost opportunities, indirect, special, incident, consequential, punitive, or any other damages whatsoever and expenses (including, without limitation, court costs and attorneys' fees) ("Losses") asserted against, resulting from, imposed upon or incurred by any of The Companies as a result of, or arising out of this agreement and/or your use of this publication. This publication is designed to provide accurate and authoritative information in regard to the subject matter covered. It is sold with the understanding that the author and publisher are not engaged in rendering legal, accounting, or other professional services. If legal advice or other expert assistance is required, the services of a competent professional person should be sought. Use of the material within this publication constitutes your acceptance of these terms.

HYPOTHETICAL PERFORMANCE RESULTS HAVE MANY INHERENT LIMITATIONS, SOME OF WHICH ARE DESCRIBED BELOW. NO REPRESENTATION IS BEING MADE THAT ANY ACCOUNT WILL OR IS LIKELY TO ACHIEVE PROFITS OR LOSSES SIMILAR TO THOSE SHOWN. IN FACT, THERE ARE FREQUENTLY SHARP DIFFERENCES BETWEEN HYPOTHETICAL PERFORMANCE RESULTS AND THE ACTUAL RESULTS SUBSEQUENTLY ACHIEVED BY ANY PARTICULAR TRADING PROGRAM.

ONE OF THE LIMITATIONS OF HYPOTHETICAL PERFORMANCE RESULTS IS THAT THEY ARE GENERALLY PREPARED WITH THE BENEFIT OF HINDSIGHT. IN ADDITION, HYPOTHETICAL TRADING DOES NOT INVOLVE FINANCIAL RISK, AND NO HYPOTHETICAL TRADING RECORD CAN COMPLETELY ACCOUNT FOR THE IMPACT OF FINANCIAL RISK IN ACTUAL TRADING. FOR EXAMPLE, THE ABILITY TO WITHSTAND LOSSES OR TO ADHERE TO A PARTICULAR TRADING PROGRAM IN SPITE OF TRADING LOSSES ARE MATERIAL POINTS WHICH CAN ALSO ADVERSELY AFFECT ACTUAL TRADING RESULTS. THERE ARE NUMEROUS OTHER FACTORS RELATED TO THE MARKETS IN GENERAL OR TO THE IMPLEMENTATION OF ANY SPECIFIC TRADING PROGRAM WHICH CANNOT BE FULLY ACCOUNTED FOR IN THE PREPARATION OF HYPOTHETICAL PERFORMANCE.

Acknowledgments

This book is a team effort, and I want to thank everybody who helped to bring this book to life:

Thank you, Liz Hester. Without your help, I would probably still be writing this book!

Special thanks to my team at Rockwell Trading: You're the best team in the world!

And I want to thank everybody in the Rockwell Family, especially my Mastermind Members and Clients, for your overwhelming response and encouragement to bring the PowerX Strategy to the world. Your feedback and the results that you achieved with this strategy inspired me to share it with others.

Last, but not least, I want to thank my children Julius and Vivian for inspiring me to be the best I can be, so I can be a great role model for you.

Table of Contents

Please Note: *There are charts and graphs used throughout this book that may be easier to understand when seen in full color. Please go **PowerXStrategy.com/gift** to download the full-color chart companion guide to this book for FREE.*

CHAPTER 1

An Epic Crash—Are You Prepared?

The Titanic was the greatest ship of its day, a feat of true architectural and engineering achievement that took the world by storm. EVERYONE wanted to be on that ship when it set sail in April 1912. The Titanic was the unsinkable ship. NOTHING could knock this luxury liner off course. From the epic staircase to the Turkish baths to the wealthiest passengers from around the world, everything about the ship was jaw-dropping.

Because the shipbuilders were so confident in the Titanic's ability to withstand anything, this "unsinkable ship" set sail with just 20 lifeboats. But no one thought twice. The Titanic was unsinkable. This was the place to be. Until it wasn't.

On the night of April 14, 1912, the Titanic hit an iceberg from its starboard side. Over the next few hours, the Titanic sank into the freezing Atlantic Ocean and over 1,500 people died.

The entire time it was sinking, no one could believe it was happening. This was the UNSINKABLE ship. This wasn't supposed to happen, now or EVER.

The captain *saw* the iceberg coming and even *watched* it smash into the side of the ship. But, by that point his hands were tied—there was nothing he could do to stop the disaster from happening.

It's the same in the market—the big guys see the crashes coming, but by the time they finally get their heads on straight, it's too late. The disaster has been struck.

In both scenarios—the Titanic crashing and major market crashes—SHOULDN'T happen. Experts believed it COULDN'T happen. But it did, it always can and *will*.

There are certain things we shouldn't roll the dice on - our safety, our lives and our wealth. The Titanic builders and passengers didn't have a backup plan because they bought into the 'unsinkable ship' hype. Ultimately leading to their untimely demise.

A Titanic Experience in the Market

We're seeing something similar in the market. Right now, we're in overbought market conditions—that means our next crash is coming. Most veteran forecasters are saying this crash is going to be unlike anything we've seen before, with numbers as high as $68 *trillion* in losses. That will wipe out millions and millions of Americans and, potentially, millions of investors around the globe.

The media outlets are also picking it up.

Bloomberg headlines, "Be Prepared for a Bear Market" and tells readers to prepare for a bear market no matter what a president does. "The President won't be able to stop the crash," they explain, "It really doesn't matter what he does."

The Street says, "An Epic Stock Market Crash Is Coming, Veteran Forecaster Peter Schiff Warns." The Economist warns that an "80% Stock Market Crash To Strike," quoting such notables as Jim Rogers, who founded the Quantum Fund with George Soros, Mark Faber, Andrew Smithers and even the Royal Bank of Scotland all warning that the Crash will be soon and be devastating. The Captains of the ship are seeing the writing on the wall, but there is still one corner saying everything is GREAT: Wall Street.

Why? They're doing it because they don't want you pulling your money out of their long-term accounts and funds. Imagine if every single customer liquidated? The market would go under instantly.

Investment firms and brokerages charge fees for every quarter your money sits with them. It's in their best interest to keep you there—and it's in their best interest to tell you the market is good and the crash rumors are just RUMORS. They are the shipbuilders saying you don't need lifeboats because *nothing bad* is going to happen.

No matter what they say, the market WILL crash. <u>We typically experience a bear market every five years—it's been almost EIGHT years without one.</u>

How does this impact YOU? You don't want to be the one going under because you failed to prepare. Even in a bear market, there are tremendous opportunities for traders and that's exactly where the PowerX Strategy comes into play. When the market crashes, you'll be zipping around the Titanic making money while every other investor drops into the icy ocean.

Market Predictors to Watch

S&P 500 Bear Markets Since WWII			
Peak	Trough	% Decline	# of Days
May 1946	Oct. 1946	-26.6%	133
June 1948	June 1949	-20.6%	363
July 1957	Oct. 1957	-20.7%	99
Jan. 1962	June 1962	-26.4%	174
Feb. 1966	Oct. 1966	-22.2%	240
Nov. 1968	May 1970	-36.1%	543
Jan. 1973	Oct. 1974	-48.2%	630
Sept. 1976	Mar. 1978	-19.4%	531
Nov. 1980	Aug. 1982	-27.1%	622
July 1987	Dec. 1987	-33.5%	101
July 1990	Oct. 1990	-19.9%	87
July 1998	Aug. 1998	-19.3%	45
Mar. 2000	Oct. 2002	-49.1%	929
Oct. 2007	Mar. 2009	-56.8%	517
Apr. 2011	Oct. 2011	-19.4%	157
Averages		-29.7%	345

This graph shows the bear markets since World War II and you can see for yourself that a bear market typically happens every five years. As you can see, this timeframe has accelerated. In 2000, the dot-com bubble burst and 49% of the market crashed. In 2007, the housing bubble burst and the market lost 56%. In April 2011, we had a small correction and the market lost 19%. **Follow the trends and it's clear to see that we're past due for a bear market.**

Take a look at the following chart of the DOW from 1995 until 2017:

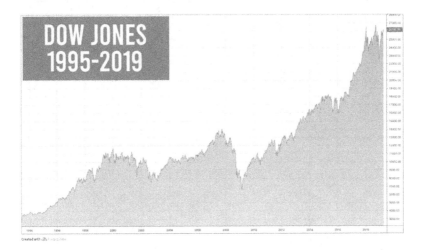

This is a monthly view beginning from 1995 through nearly the end of 2017. Starting in 1995, the market was going up. We had a small correction in 1998, but after, it moves higher and higher. Then 2000 comes around—and you know what happens then. Everything changed and the market bottomed out, dropping 48% in a matter of months.

It took *eight years* for the DOW to recover. Then, just when we're able to restore the market, the housing market crashes and prices sink *again*. Then they climb, until the mini-recession in 2011 happens and down we go...*again*.

While there was a little correction in 2011 and some volatility in 2015 and 2016, since 2009, the DOW has been growing steadily. At the time of the writing of this book, we're at an all-time high and *keep* hitting new all-time highs.

No matter how you look at it, the cycle stays consistent—we move up, we have a little correction, we move up more and everyone assumes the market is going to keep going in the right direction. But, soon enough, there's another crash—history always repeats itself.

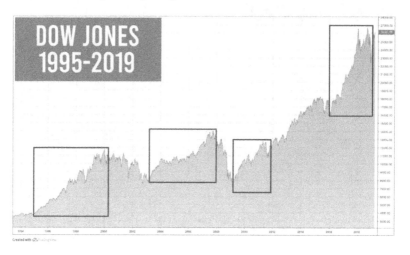

Can you see how the current pattern matches the last 2 crashes? And we are overdue for a correction!

There's a silver lining to all of this, however. With the PowerX Strategy, you could potentially make money before, during and after a crash. When everyone else is losing their retirement and savings to the icy deeps, you'll be actively trading your account and can *profit on the volatility of the markets.*

Let's face it, we're *all* on the stock market Titanic. Every single one of us, including me, is headed toward the next iceberg on this chart. But we don't have to crash. We can get on a speedboat and zip around taking gains while others crash and sink their financial ship.

So how do you get aboard the speedboat?

Your ticket is the PowerX Strategy. Unlike the vast majority of Wall Street-reliant investors, you won't be tied to the actions of the entire market and go down with that ship. You'll be involved in, often unknown, individual stocks that yield profits speedily in both directions: UP and DOWN.

It all starts here with the PowerX Strategy. You CAN make money in the market if you have:

1. A Proven Trading Strategy
2. A Solid Trading Plan
3. The <u>Discipline</u> to follow your strategy—that means putting in the time, which is doable in just 15 minutes per day

We'll cover these in detail in this book. You'll also learn the secrets from starting small to growing big and even bigger still. And how, if you know your numbers and can learn and grow from your mistakes, *you can have what you need to succeed as a trader.*

This trading approach will help you check your boxes. By tapping into PowerX you can…

- ☐ Grow your wealth
- ☐ Protect yourself from the crash—a crash that's ALWAYS COMING
- ☐ Gain security for you and your family, by gaining *financial freedom* once and for all
- ☐ Learn how to build a legacy for your family that extends to your children, your grandchildren *and beyond*

I'll warn you now, it won't always be easy. However, it is very doable. The people who tell you it's not possible to make money through all cycles of the market are the people who can't hack it themselves. They don't have a proven trading strategy like you'll now have.

With PowerX, you'll have tools, resources and the direction to do this. I'll be here every step of the way, helping you get where you want to be.

Welcome Aboard!

Who am I?
And Why Should You Listen to Me?

My name is Markus Heitkoetter and I came to the U.S. from Germany in 2002. At the time, I had $30,000 in my pocket. Today, I'm a multi-millionaire.

My approach is simple, straightforward and, if you follow it to the letter, you can change your life. It's completely focused on getting you to your goal of financial independence through consistent, long-term wealth.

So, how are we going to flip the switch and take you from where you are today to where you want to be tomorrow? By turning into a smart, strategic, systematic trader starting NOW. My PowerX Strategy is for newer traders, experienced traders and even those who know nothing about trading. More than 461,752 people have requested to learn about my strategies over the past decade. And now I'm sharing them with YOU!

I started trading in the late 1980s when I was in high school. Back then, if you wanted to buy stock, you needed to go to a bank. I went to Deutsche Bank and opened a trading account with my hard-earned teenage life savings— 50 Deutsche Mark (DM), equal to about $50 at the time.

My method? I asked the guy at the bank what I could afford. Not really the most strategic approach, but I bought one share of Volkswagen stock.

The next day, I inserted 20 cents in the payphone at school and called my banker.

"How's my stock doing?" I asked.

"Well, it's now trading at 50.20 DM," he said. I was thrilled! I had *made money* in the stock market without doing anything. I didn't care that it was 20 cents. I was 20 cents richer than I'd been the day before. I was on my way to actual profits. It was truly one of the greatest thrills of my life.

A few hours later, I called again.

"How's my stock doing?" I asked, again.

"We're up to 50.35 DM," he said. That night at home, I called again.

"We closed at 50.40 DM," the banker told me. I went to sleep that night in a state of total bliss. I am a trader, I thought, as I drifted off to sleep. I am making money RIGHT NOW.

On day three, I called again.

"Markus," the banker asked, "how much money are you hoping to make from this trade?" I thought about it.

"10 DM," I replied, decidedly.

"So 20%? That's your goal?"

"Yes." I couldn't tell quite where he was going.

"I will make that happen. Come to the bank after school today and I'll give you 10 DM. Just STOP CALLING ME!!"

You've made your first profitable trade, I thought. It didn't matter that the 10 DM was meant to cool my constant calling. I didn't care. All I could see was potential—and PROFIT.

What I Wanted vs. What I Did

After high school, I prepared to make the leap and trade full-time—but my parents weren't exactly thrilled with the prospect. Having a banker give you 10 DM to go away and launching a successful financial career are two very different things. I couldn't see it though, all I could see was the .40 profit I'd made in a matter of *days* on my single Volkswagen stock.

Ultimately, I took the safe, responsible route. I went to college and got a job at IBM. I gave up on my dream because I didn't have support from others—and I'll always regret that. The more people I talk to at my international events and seminars, the more I hear similar experiences—people who wanted to try something new or follow their passion or get into trading but, because others pushed back on them, they got back on the traditional straight and narrow, like I did.

I worked my way up the IBM corporate ladder quickly, carving out a path for myself in their global services consulting division. I was traveling the world for my job and staying in the finest hotels in the world. Flying first class and driving BMWs when I touched down. On the surface, I was living the life, but it had a price. I was working 6-7 dyas, 60 to 80 hours per week. I was tired, pushed to the max and burned out.

I'll never forget the moment, I was sitting in a five-star hotel room in Vienna after a very long day. The lights were dim and the air was stuffy and stank of hotel cleaners and it was quiet. Too quiet. Back home, everyone was celebrating a friend's birthday and no one had even invited me. My friends and family had stopped inviting me because I always said no. I *always* had to work.

Sitting there alone it hit me. I had no time for family or friends. No hobbies. No passions. I had the golden handcuffs that were keeping me tethered to this job. What was I doing with my life? And, was THIS it?

Mergers and Finding My Meaning

Just then I got a call. IBM, the company I'd given everything to, was merging with Pricewaterhouse Coopers and 4,600 jobs would be eliminated immediately. Sure, I was a loyal and hardworking employee, but in these situations even I was replaceable. I'd given everything to the company and it now seemed I was on the brink of losing even *this*. It was my lowest low and even though I didn't know how, I knew I needed out. I needed my life back.

I finally saw the trap! I was trading time for money. While the money was good, I sacrificed everything I had and my future to get that money. **I was on professional autopilot. I wasn't living, I was simply alive.**

I wanted to live a life filled with the people, places and *experiences* that mattered. I was done working 10-12 hour days driving someone else's dream. I wanted freedom. **I wanted to find myself and MY life.**

In 2002, I packed my things, said my goodbyes and moved 5,480 miles from Munich to Austin, Texas. When I got there, I told myself I would go all-in on my high school dream. I had been trading since High School, but not full time. I knew if I had more time I could make it work.

I got to Texas with $30,000 in my pocket. Of that, I committed $20,000 to a trading account. I was ecstatic. Now I could finally follow my passion! Little did I know my dreams were about to be crushed again.

The Market Crushed Me

This isn't some fairytale and I'm not a mythical hero, believe me! I didn't plunk down my $20,000 and watch it grow and grow as I rode off into the sunset. I didn't turn $20,000 into $200,000 into $2 million overnight.

Nope. I got CRUSHED. Within a few weeks, my account was already down, and after a few more months I had lost more than half of my account. Suddenly, I had no clue what to do.

This wasn't like I'd remembered. Where were the daily gains on my Volkswagen stock? Where was the limitless potential? The excitement? The massive revenue potential?

In an instant, I'd given up my lucrative job, moved to another country and poured all of the money I'd allocated for my goals into an account that, now, was on a downward free fall despite my spending 10-plus hours each day tied to the computer.

I'd given myself a year to figure it all out and just four months in I couldn't imagine having eight more months in me—mentally, emotionally or financially.

My AHA Moment

I'll never forget the moment, I was sitting there at the dark kitchen table, my head in my hands, staring at my logs and account with that sick feeling in my stomach. *This is it*, I thought. *This is the breaking point and I don't know what I can do to keep myself from going back into the golden handcuffs.*

Then suddenly I saw it, like a neon sign in the dark. I stared at my logs and the answer stared back at me. I saw what I'd been doing wrong and how to fix it. I was shocked back to reality. Reinvigorated, I applied those "aha" ideas to my trading the very next day. Within a few months, I was profitable.

I wouldn't have to go back to IBM or find another soul-crushing 9-to-5. I could have my life and my trading business and strike a balance that worked for ME.

Underscoring it all, I could have lasting financial freedom—true wealth that could define my lifestyle, for me and my family, now and in the future.

During this rollercoaster period, I continued to remind myself of one core tenet of my trading business and my life.

Trading equals freedom.

I'll say it again,

Trading equals FREEDOM.

There <u>will</u> be challenges. You <u>will</u> lose money sometimes. Some days it will be VERY hard. You will have to deal with the naysayers, critics and the self-doubt that creeps in when you least expect it.

But, at the end of the day, <u>trading equals freedom</u>. Freedom from "The Man." Freedom from the grind. Freedom from relying on a paycheck. Freedom from the nagging fears about your finances, your family and your future. I craved freedom, and I got it. I want that for you.

What emerged from that period was a tried, tested and true system that's helped me take control of my financial future by maximizing opportunity and mitigating risk.

The principles underlying the PowerX Strategy were crafted during that early period in Austin and are exactly how I've grown my own accounts as I've pursued my passion for trading and living life on my terms.

Bringing the PowerX Strategy to Life

My goal, now, is to bring the PowerX Strategy to others. I figured out the market secrets that work for me, and now I have the freedom I've always wanted. It's time for me to pay it forward to you.

Now it's your turn. You have no excuse NOT to dive in. I get it—fear, anxiety and a lack of self-confidence can hold you back. We've been conditioned to follow the straight and narrow—to go to college, get a respectable job, earn a consistent paycheck and, eventually, to retire on a fixed income. It doesn't matter if we like it or even WANT it. That's the "dream." But, let's be honest, how "dreamy" does that sound to you?

If that sounds familiar—if you're living a life you don't love—STOP IT NOW!

You have the power to change EVERYTHING for the better. You have the power to uplevel your game and, finally, free yourself from the golden handcuffs keeping you in your grind of a job.

You can do this. Trading can equal freedom for you, too. And when it does, you will never look back.

Except to ask yourself, "Why didn't I do this *sooner?*"

CHAPTER 2

What is the PowerX Strategy?

The PowerX Strategy is a TRADING strategy, NOT an investment strategy.

What is Trading?

First of all, here's what trading is NOT:

- **Trading does NOT mean sitting in front of your computer all day.**

  There's a myth that traders are sitting in front of their computer all day or all night watching the markets like a hawk. Even though this might be true for some traders, this is NOT what we are talking about here. Once you learn how to trade the PowerX Strategy, you only need about 15 minutes per day.

- **Trading does NOT mean analyzing balance sheets and weird ratios.**

  When trading, you mainly rely on indicators to make a decision. When using the PowerX Strategy, you are only holding a position for 5-20 days. You're NOT looking for a stock to 10x. All you want, is a stock that is ready to move 5 - 15% in the next few weeks. Therefore, you don't have to analyze balance sheets, profit and loss statements, P/E ratios, Market Capitalization, etc. All you need is to know how to look at a chart in a certain way. You will learn exactly how to do that in a later chapter.

So what IS trading?

- **Trading, very simply, means taking control of your financial future by *actively* buying and selling stocks or options.**

  To be successful, you need the handful of resources and tools I will teach you about throughout the book.

- **Trading means checking your account every day-for as little as 15 minutes - and taking action.**

  Remember the Titanic? You want to react BEFORE hitting the iceberg. And that's what active trading is all about. You are checking your positions every night and making decisions for the next day.

- **Trading means leveraging a proven strategy to grow your account.**

   And the PowerX Strategy you are about to learn is exactly that: A proven trading strategy that can help you to take your account to the next level.

Important: I don't want you to think you're going to make $10,000 your first day trading - unless you're trading a $1,000,000 account!

I've had plenty of big profit days, but trading is not some get-rich-quick scheme. If someone tells you it's an overnight ticket to millionaire status, run far and run fast.

Success in trading relies on smart strategies and builds on relatively small earnings in the beginning. Those small earnings continue to fuel your portfolio and enable you to sharpen your skills and refine your approach. One trade isn't going to make you rich. Consistency is more important than just "one lucky trade." Focus on small and consistent profits, and over time you will see fantastic results.

The best traders exhibit those qualities every day. They're completely disciplined in their approach and focus on the long-term. By being consistent and decisive, you'll be in a good position to grow your trading business, driving wealth and success today and tomorrow. But you need to invest time, discipline and patience, plus the knowledge I'll share in the coming chapters. Do that, and you'll increase the odds of making money in the markets.

Ultimately, trading is like a chess game. You need to be focused and always thinking several steps ahead. If you can do that - and you will be able to with the PowerX Strategy —you'll be able to make quick decisions and grow your account consistently.

What Makes the PowerX Strategy So Powerful?

If you want to be successful as a trader, you MUST have a proven trading strategy. Without a strategy, you will fail.

If you google "trading strategy", you will see that there are over 6,020,000 results! So how do you find the "best" trading strategy for you?

Here is my criteria for a great trading strategy:

1. **Easy to learn and understand**

   A great trading strategy should be easy to learn and understand. If you can't explain a trading strategy in 5 minutes or less, it's too complicated. A proven trading strategy uses very few rules to cut down on error. And as you will see, the PowerX Strategy has only 3 rules.

2. **Simple to execute**

   A great trading strategy has clear-cut rules that leave no room for interpretation. It allows you to apply the rules and instantly make a decision - no second guessing. When using the PowerX Strategy, you will be able to make a decision in 30 seconds or less. It's that powerful.

3. **Works for beginners and experienced investors**
   A great trading strategy should be a good fit for both beginners and experienced investors. Why would you need a different trading strategy when you become more experienced? A great trading strategy should work for any experience level and any account size.

4. **Start small, grow big**
   A great trading strategy should work for both small and large accounts. You should be able to trade a strategy on a small account of $2,000 and use the same trading strategy to trade a larger account. The PowerX Strategy is designed to work well whether your account is $2,000, $20,000, $200,000 or $2,000,000.

5. **Spend minutes, not hours**
   In my opinion, a great trading strategy shouldn't require you to sit in front of your computer all day long. After all, you probably have a life outside of trading: You still might have a job, or maybe you're running a business or you're retired.
   That's why the PowerX Strategy only requires you to fire up the computer for about 15 minutes every day to make your trading decisions for the next day.

There's one more advantage to using the PowerX Strategy for your trading: **It uses technical indicators.**

Indicators are based on technical analysis, **a scientific approach to trade the markets.** The idea is that all information is already factored into the current prices.

Another idea is that the past price action is somewhat indicative of future moves, i.e. if a stock has been trading sideways in the past 12 months, it is more likely to keep trading sideways.

Please note that I said "more likely". Of course, it could start to trend but the basic idea is that stocks have certain predictive characteristics.

Take a look at the chart below:

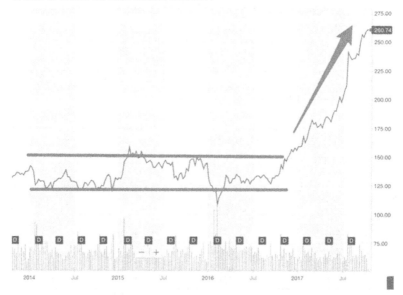

As you can see, for years this stock has been trading in a range between $120 - $150. Therefore, it was more likely to go sideways. And once the stock started trending, it's now more likely to keep trending.

You can use indicators to easily predict the moves of a stock, and in the next chapter you will learn how.

When using indicators, for the most part, you don't have to worry about the news and how to interpret it. You don't have to worry about reading through complicated earnings statements trying to understand what the company is planning to do.

The PowerX Strategy is a powerful trading strategy that's perfect for beginners as well as experienced traders. It fits all of my criteria for a great strategy and uses only technical indicators which is by far my most favored approach.

Before we get into indicators, it's important to understand the "3 Keys to Trading Success":

1. Find the best stocks
2. Limit your risk
3. Take your profits

Because we've laid the groundwork previously, you should have a good sense of why these steps are so important and how, together, they make trading a smart, profitable and streamlined approach to generating wealth.

Don't overthink these steps. They seem simple and straightforward because they ARE simple and straightforward. Keep that mindset. The more you look for deeper meaning or assume that there's some other secret step to it all and over-complicate it, the worse off you're going to be.

To be successful as a trader, you need to find the best stocks, limit your risk and take your profits. That's IT.

Key 1: Find the Best Stocks

Even if you want to trade options, you need to find the best stocks first, because options are bound to the underlying stock!

The key is to find stocks that are ready to move. You may have heard the saying: *The trend is your friend.* Well, it's no different with the PowerX Strategy. It identifies the shorter-term trends and seeks to get aboard that next swing in the stock's price for profits.

When stocks START moving, they have a high likelihood of CONTINUING to move. There are three indicators the PowerX Strategy focuses on to identify these stocks. I chose these three indicators because aside from being consistently effective when used properly, as you'll see, they're easy to use—WAY easier than all the complicated chart formations and caps and head and shoulders and triangles, etc. Later in the book, we'll dive into these three indicators.

When you find a stock that's ready to move, that means its option price is ready to move, too.

Here's an example:

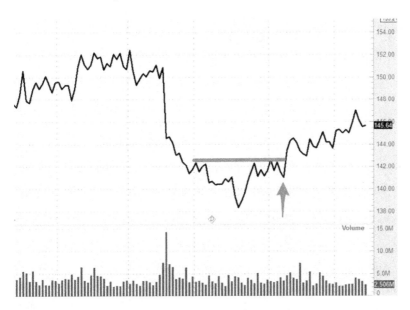

As you can see, the trend of the stock was moving down, then it moved sideways for a few days, and then it finally broke out and moved higher.

Here's another example:

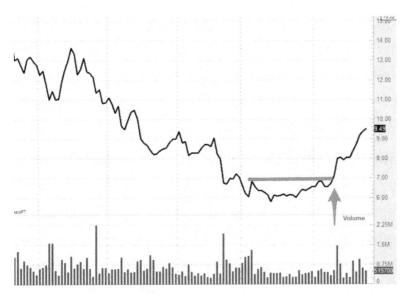

Similar to the previous example, the stock trend was going down, then it moved sideways for a couple of weeks, and now it's breaking out of the consolidation and starts trending up.

We'll discuss identifying these trends in the next chapter. When determining which stocks to evaluate, I started with analyzing the DOW 30. I would look at each stock to determine if there was a trending opportunity. This can be time consuming to evaluate each stock individually so I created my PowerX software to do the heavy lifting for me and expand my search to all available stocks automatically. It provides me with the best opportunities as per the PowerX strategy to evaluate.

It's important for us to lay the groundwork first so that when we get to the tactical step-by-steps, you understand what we're doing, why we're doing it and what we hope to achieve by following this process. With a solid foundation, you can build your business without uncertainty, self-doubt and anxiety. This foundation and understanding will give you confidence in your trading and help you to grow your account consistently without the fear.

Key 2: Limit Your Risk (Golden Rule)

Our goal with the PowerX Strategy is to find high probability and low-risk trades. Too often, people select stocks or options based on their "gut" or because they like the company. Here's the thing—as **"good" as your gut may be, there's no room for it in trading.**

As traders, we want to be data-driven and deliberate so we can **limit risk and increase profit scientifically.** The numbers tell the story no matter the company or the market conditions. Follow the numbers, and you'll automatically reduce your risk.

When it comes to risk, this is very important so please never forget: We're always seeking to RISK $1 to MAKE $2. That's my GOLDEN RULE!

Even before entering a trade, by employing my Golden Rule, you'll have a maximum predefined amount of risk and a predefined profit target. You'll know when to exit with a profit. Armed with the numbers to help you, you'll be able to resist the urge to stay in "just a little longer" to try to find some off-the-charts fortune your gut tells you is right around the corner. Those urges are bad business.

By leaning on this Golden Rule, **you'll avoid one major slip up many traders make—holding onto a trade for too long.** If you hold on in your greed, you could lose a big chunk of money on a single trade or over the span of a few trades. Either way, it's NOT what we want—and it could put you out of business fast.

In addition to my Golden Rule, in the beginning, I suggest that you follow a **2% Rule: "Never risk more than 2% of your account on any given trade."**

The 2% rule is critical when you are just getting started or working with a small account.

For example, take Amy, a single, homeschooling mom and a close, personal friend who called me a few weeks ago.

She asked me, "Markus, I know that you're doing stock trading, so let me ask you, is it really possible to make money? And, do you think *I* should trade?

I'm asking, because here's my situation. I only have $5,000 in my savings account. I know I should have more money, but that's what it is right now. It's all I have, and honestly, I can't afford to lose that money."

I said, "Amy, yes! I think you should be trading. The money sitting in your savings account isn't doing anything for you. In fact, with inflation as it is, your money is actually melting away sitting there. I know it can be scary to risk that money, so here's what I suggest; apply the 2% Rule.

This means, you only risk 2% on any given trade. For example, 2% of $5,000 = $100. You would not want to risk any more than that on a trade. Let me explain why.

Let's say that you have 10 losing trades in a row, which is pretty unlikely, but possible. After 10 losing trades in a row, you're down $1,000, but you still have $4,000, and what you learned from those losing trades. You still have money left to implement the adjustments you need to make. You're not wiped out!"

I'm giving you the same advice I gave my personal friend. And even though I suggest you begin with the 2% rule, once you have a good track record, in order to grow your account, you may need to expand on that rule based on your account size and overall risk tolerance. We'll talk more about this in Chapter 6.

You can also use options to help manage risk. Later in this book, I'll walk you through the options trading process step by step. For now, though, let's focus on how this approach will manage risk as you buy and sell stocks.

Key 3: Take Your Profits

As obvious as it might sound, **NOT taking profits is one of the biggest mistakes I see traders make.**

You know what to do when the trade goes against you. In this section, we'll discuss what to do when the trade moves in your favor. This is extremely important!

If a trade goes in the right direction, you need to know when to take your profit. **You must take profits while they are there because the markets can turn around quickly.**

Keep in mind: <u>Nobody ever went broke taking profits.</u>

Let me show you two examples.

The first one is Twitter (TWTR). Twitter had an IPO in 2013, and on the first day, shares of Twitter soared 73% above the offering price. The stock went from $26 to $45. I remember friends who were calling me saying, "Oh my God! I got in and I almost doubled my money!"

And they were right, they *would have* doubled their money because in the next few days, Twitter went from $26 all the way to $65. However, afterwards it went all the way down to right around $18. and they had never taken profits! They were still greedily holding the stocks. The determining factor in whether this was a great trade or a losing trade is *when you exited*. **You need to know when to take your money off the table.**

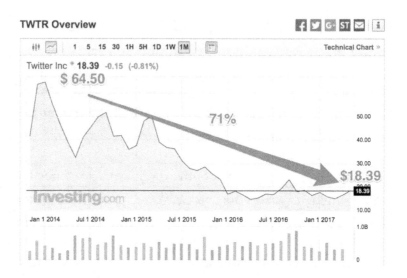

The second example is SnapChat (SNAP). In 2017, Snapchat had an IPO, and a similar thing happened. The day of the IPO, prices skyrocketed. Everybody loved Snapchat, and the stock went up 44% on the first day.

Over the next few days, prices moved even higher, all the way to $27.09. But then in less than 6 months, SNAP dropped to $14.89.

This is why it is so important to take profits while they are there.

So the question is:
When exactly should you take profits?

Here's what I do: "The Golden Rule." I mentioned it in the last section but I want to get into more detail.

Remember "The Golden Rule" is 1:2. For every one dollar that you risk, you try to make two. Not three, not four, not five. The rule is simple: for every $1 you risk, you try to make $2 or for every $10 that you risk, you try to make $20.

Here's an example:

If a stock is trading at $100, and you're willing to risk $10, you would exit the trade as soon as the price drops to $90.

And when the price moves up to $120, you exit the trade.

In the next chapter, I will show you a formula to determine the "best" stop loss and profit target as we use "The Golden Rule" of 1:2.

You might wonder: What if the stock keeps going up? Shouldn't I try to stay in this trade?

Based on my experience: NO!

As soon as you hit your profit target, don't look at the stock anymore. Because it doesn't matter if it goes up to $130, $140, or $150. Don't try to make a home run trade, because more often than not, it doesn't work.

Success often comes through smaller, more consistent wins. If you can risk $10 and make $20 consistently, you make money with trading.

The best part about this rule?

If you apply "The Golden Rule", you can make money even if you're wrong half of the time.

Let me show you how.

Let's say you're risking $100 on a trade. This means your profit target is $200.

In this example, you're placing 10 trades.

Out of these 10 trades, five trades are losing trades. So you lose $500 (5 * $100).

The other five trades are winning trades. You make $1,000 (5 * $200.)

How much money do you have after 10 trades? $500!

THIS is why exits are more important than the entries. For me, this was a game changer, and here's why: **I know my risk and reward before I even enter my trade.** This helps me to <u>reduce stress and emotions</u> like greed and fear which every trader wrestles with. I <u>use science and numbers to eliminate them from the equation</u> and therefore reduce my risk and take profits while they are still there.

Most traders have it wrong. They're only focusing on the entry. They want to time the entry perfectly! And once they are in the trade, they exhale and don't worry about the trade any more. But that's wrong!

The *exit* of a trade is more important than the entry. A monkey can enter the market. **Money is made and lost when you exit the market!**

But it gets even better. **When you know your exits before you even enter the trade, you can put the trade on autopilot!** Every broker allows you to automatically apply a stop loss to exit the trade when it is going against you. You can also place a profit target that automatically exits the trade for a profit when it is moving in your favor.

This way, you don't have to watch your stocks throughout the day.

In the next chapter, I will show you how the PowerX Strategy uses these powerful principles and combines them into a powerful trading strategy.

CHAPTER 3

The PowerX Strategy

Please Note: There are charts and graphs used throughout this book that may be easier to understand when seen in full color. Please go to **PowerXStrategy.com/gift** to download the full-color chart companion guide to this book for FREE.

Let's dive right into the real meat and potatoes of this book. Let's talk about the PowerX Strategy, a powerful strategy for trading stocks and options.

With this strategy, you can make money even if you're wrong 50% of the time. Think about that...

Where else can you be wrong HALF of the time and still make thousands—or even MILLIONS?

I can't think of one thing. Except trading.

The PowerX Strategy focuses on finding stocks on the move, like I mentioned in the last chapter. The more explosive the movement, the better. Why is it better? Because we can profit more quickly and move on to the next opportunity.

These stocks, as you'll soon see, have the highest profit potential. By entering at the right time and knowing when to exit profitably and when to exit with a loss, you'll be able to start trading for a part-time or maybe even full-time income.

Part 1: Setting Up Your Charts

As I previously explained, I believe in technical analysis and indicators because they are scientific and take the guesswork out of my trading. In a moment, you will see how easy it is to identify trends using indicators. When using technical analysis, you need a charting software.

As I said, I developed software for my use to scan over 15,000 stocks and options with the PowerX strategy and returns the picks of the day to me in minutes.

While many brokerage firms offer charting software for free, you are required to look at the stocks and options one at a time, which is not only extremely time consuming, you also have to know which stocks to look at and often my best picks have been stocks I've never even heard of before.

If you don't have a charting software yet, you can simply use finance.yahoo.com.

These are the settings I use with the following indicators:

- Slow Stochastics with the setting of 14, 3 and 3
- RSI (Relative Strength Index) with a setting of 7
- MACD with a setting of 12, 26 and 9

Most charting software on the market has these indicators with these settings available. By using these three indicators simultaneously, you'll improve your accuracy and be able to make better decisions as a trader. Use one indicator and you run the risk of getting false signals. Using three is your own personal checks and balances system. Each confirms—or calls into question—the others, ensuring you're on the right path.

When you load a chart of a symbol, it might look like THIS:

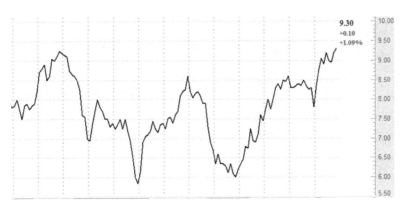

At first glance, THIS stock looks like a poor prospect...if you invest with the hold and hope method. This stock moved all over the place and is barely higher than it was one year ago; 12 months ago, this stock was trading at $8.00 and now it is trading at $9.30.

If you followed a "buy-and-hold" approach, you would have had a few heart attacks along the way. The stock moved from $8.00 to $9.50 for a 19% gain, then dropped to $6.00 for a 37% loss. Then it moved back up to $8.50 gaining 42% then dropped back down to $6.00 for another loss of 29%. It's quite the roller coaster! Now… overall, you would have had a 16% increase for the 12 months if you held on for the ride but was the emotional impact of riding that roller coaster worth it?

On the other hand, what if you could eliminate the emotional roller coaster and take control of your money instead of feeling like you are at the mercy of the market?

If you traded this stock according to the PowerX Strategy, you could have made 61% and saved yourself a lot of stress and heartache. Here's how…

FIRST, we need to change the chart to a Open-High-Low-Close or "OHLC Chart."

This means that instead of a solid line, we are seeing bars with a notch on the left side, which shows the opening price of the day, and a notch on the right side, which shows the close of the day.

Here's how to read what's called an Open-High-Low-Close bar:

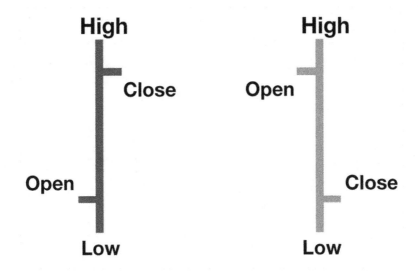

When we switch our chart to a bar chart, it looks like this:

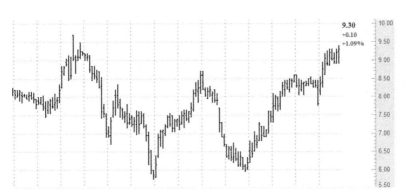

Now it's time to add our technical indicators.

Indicator 1: Slow Stochastic (Stochastic %K)

The first indicator we want to add to the chart is the "Slow Stochastic." In some charting software packages, this indicator is also called "Stochastic %K."

We add Stochastic %K with a parameter of **14 and 3** to our chart. It is displayed at the bottom.

Stochastic K is an oscillator that moves between 0 and 100. We want to **pay close attention to the bold 50 line**. This indicator has been added to the bottom of this chart.

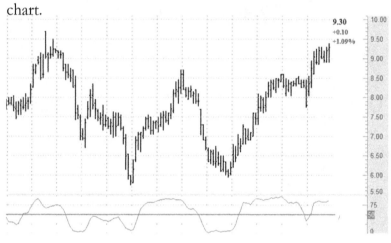

*Please go to **PowerXStrategy.com/gift** to download the full-color chart companion guide to this book for FREE.*

Whenever the Stochastic %K is ABOVE 50 and rising, it's indicating that the stock is in an **uptrend** (see shaded area below).

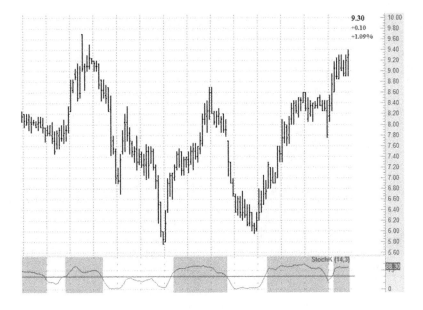

And when the Stochastic %K is BELOW 50 and falling, it's indicating that the stock is in a **downtrend** (see shaded area below).

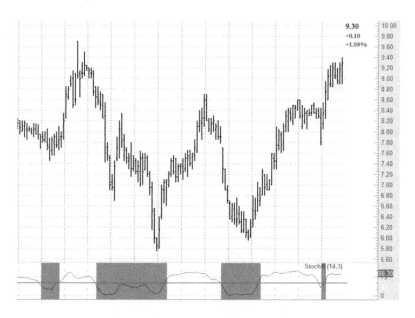

As traders, we don't want to rely on only ONE indicator because it could give us many false signals since all indicators are flawed to a degree. We want to increase overall performance by adding two more indicators.

In my years of trading, I found that using three indicators is perfect:

- When using *less* than three indicators, you're getting too many false signals.
- When using *more* than three indicators, you're getting conflicting signals.

In my experience, three indicators are the magic number to get the highest accuracy.

So, let's move on to the next indicator.

Indicator 2: Relative Strength Index (RSI)

The next indicator is the Relative Strength Index (RSI), and we are using a setting of 7.

Same as Stochastic %K, the RSI Indicator is range-bound and oscillates between 0 and 100.

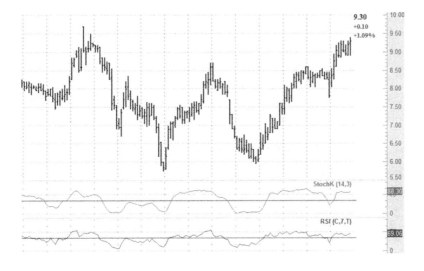

*Please go to **PowerXStrategy.com/gift** to download the full-color chart companion guide to this book for FREE.*

Again, we want to **pay attention to the 50 line**. When the RSI is ABOVE 50 and rising, it's indicating that the stock is in an **uptrend** (see shaded area below).

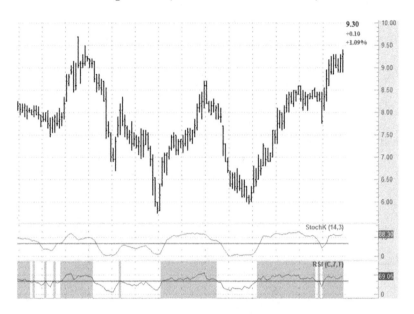

When the RSI is BELOW 50 and falling, it's indicating the stock is in a **downtrend** (see shaded area below).

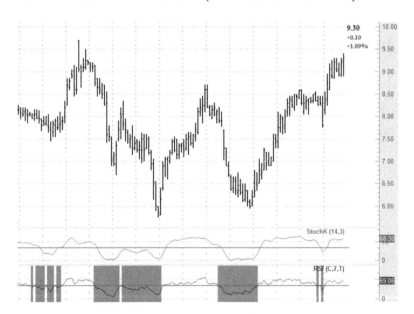

Indicator 3: Moving Average Convergence Divergence (MACD)

The third indicator that we want to add to the chart is the Moving Average Convergence Divergence (MACD). We use the settings of **MACD (12, 26, 9)**.

The MACD consists of three components:

- The MACD itself (blue line)
- The Signal Line (purple line)
- A Histogram shows the difference between the MACD and its Signal Line.
  Note: The Histogram will show in most charting software as part of the MACD but we do not specifically use it for the PowerX Strategy.

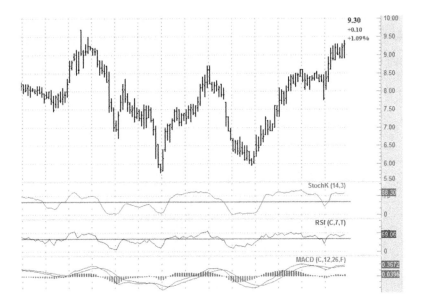

Please go to **PowerXStrategy.com/gift** *to download the full-color chart companion guide to this book for FREE.*

When the MACD is ABOVE its Signal Line and rising, it's indicating that the stock is in an **uptrend** (see shaded area below).

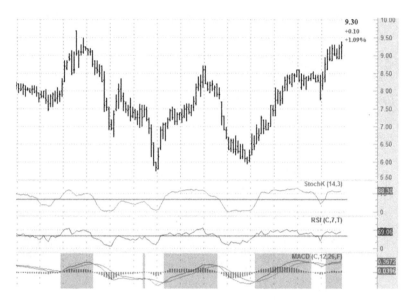

When the MACD is BELOW its Signal Line and falling, it's indicating that the stock is in a **downtrend** (see shaded area below).

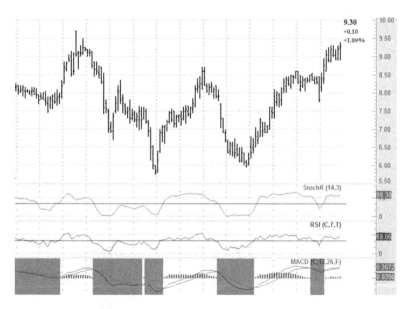

Now let's bring this all together. In the chart below you'll see all indicators together:

- When <u>all three</u> indicators are "green" (above the line), the stock is in an **uptrend**.
- When <u>all three</u> indicators are "red" (below the line), the stock is in a **downtrend**.

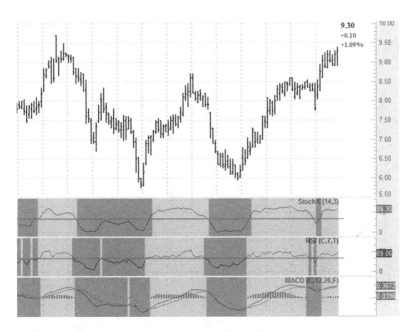

I personally like to make this even easier to see, and here's how:

- When <u>all three</u> indicators are green, I color the bars in the chart **green**.
- When <u>all three</u> indicators are red, I color the bars in the chart **red**.
- When only 1 or 2 indicators are green or red, i.e. not all three, then I color the bars in the chart **black**.

Some software programs allow for bar coloring while others do not.

This makes it VERY easy for me to see when a stock is in an **uptrend** (green bars), when it is in a **downtrend** (red bars), and when it is only moving **sideways** (black bars).

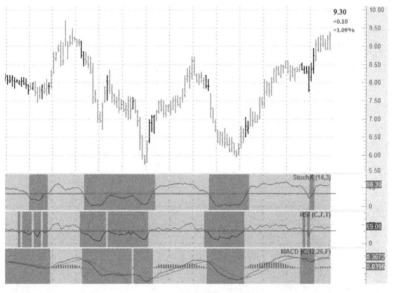

With these settings, **you can now determine in 5 seconds or less, whether a stock is in an uptrend or a downtrend.** Just look at the previous image.

SO... is this stock currently in an uptrend or in a downtrend?

- The Slow Stochastic %K is at 88.3, i.e. ABOVE 50
- The RSI is at 69.06, i.e. ABOVE 50
- The MACD is ABOVE its Signal Line

*Please go to **PowerXStrategy.com/gift** to download the full-color chart companion guide to this book for FREE.*

Since all three indicators are showing an uptrend, this stock is in an uptrend right now.

Easy enough, isn't it?

In the next section, you will learn how we use this information to determine when exactly to buy and sell this stock. And in Chapter 5, you'll learn how to use this chart to trade options. It all starts here with these 3 simple indicators.

Making sense?

Then let's move on.

Part 2: When to Enter a Trade

In this section, you will learn when exactly to BUY a stock and when to SELL it.

The best part? Since we've done all of the prep work, this step is very simple and straightforward.

Here are the rules:

#1. We want to BUY a stock $0.01 <u>above the high</u> of the bar on which all three indicators are green, i.e. the first green bar.

Here's an example:

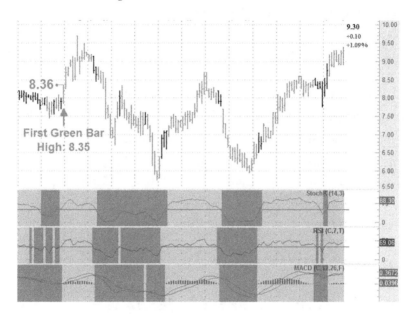

The high of the first green bar is at $8.35, therefore, we want to BUY $0.01 above that high at $8.36.

As you can see, we're getting filled on the next day because the stock price proceeded to move higher the following morning.

*Please go to **PowerXStrategy.com/gift** to download the full-color chart companion guide to this book for FREE.*

Here's another example:

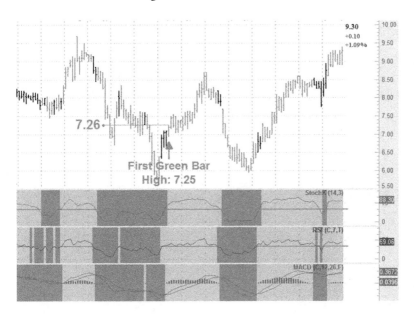

The high of the first green bar is at $7.25, therefore, we want to BUY $0.01 above that high at $7.26.

And again, we're getting filled on the next day.

Here's an example where we don't get filled right away:

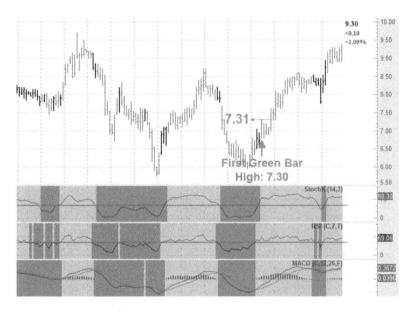

The high of the first green bar is at $7.30, therefore, we want to BUY $0.01 above that high at $7.31.

But for the next three days, the stock doesn't move above $7.30. But since the bars are still green—in other words, all three indicators are still signaling BUY—we leave the order in the market. On the 4th day after the signal occurred, the stock finally moves higher and we get filled.

IMPORTANT: If we had gotten a BLACK bar, we would have canceled the order and waited for the next green bar before considering to enter a bullish trade.

We want to SELL a stock $0.01 below the low of the bar on which all three indicators are red—in other words, below the first red bar.

SHORTING a stock is a term that applies when we decide to sell a stock without owning it. Effectively, it is a bet against the stock price. As in, we anticipate that a stock price is about to fall so we sell it now and plan to buy it back later at a lower price to realize our profits. SHORTING may be a new concept if you're new to trading but it is very common in the the markets and has been around for over a century. If you want to SHORT a stock that's a bearish lean, you can use the same logic to SELL a stock or you can purchase Put options that would allow you to profit from the decline of the stock's price.

Here's an example:

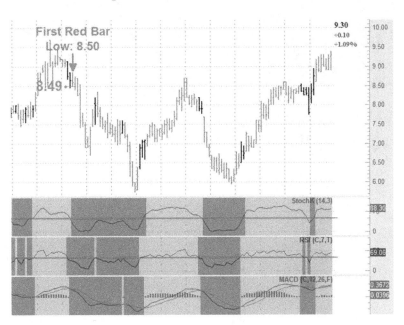

The low of the first red bar is at $8.50, therefore, we want to SELL $0.01 below that low at $8.49.

And we're getting filled on the next day because we can see that the stock price continued to fall the following day.

A few weeks later, we get another signal:

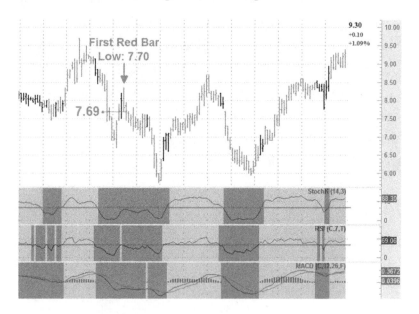

The low of the first red bar is at $7.70, therefore, we want to SELL $0.01 below that low at $7.69.

And we're getting filled on the next day.

There are two more SHORT signals. Take a look at the image below:

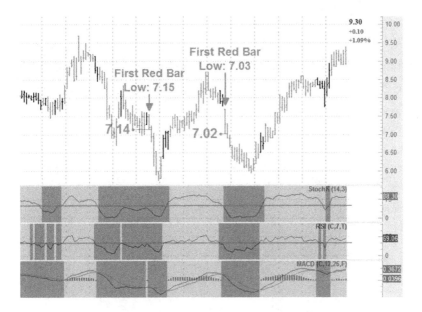

*Please go to **PowerXStrategy.com/gift** to download the full-color chart companion guide to this book for FREE.*

So in total, we get eight trading signals:

- Four BUY Signals and
- Four SELL SHORT Signals, if you like to SELL stocks

Here are all the signals in one chart—note, GREEN upward triangles are BUY signals and RED downward triangles are SELL signals.

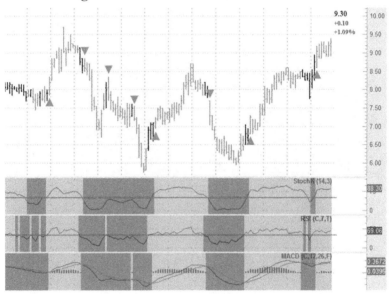

One critical part of the PowerX Strategy is that we do not enter when we're too late to the party! **We only take the FIRST entry signal into a trend.** You need to wait for a green bar, and then try to enter $0.01 above the high of that bar. <u>If you miss this entry, for whatever reason, you should wait for the next entry signal. Never chase a trade!</u> If you missed it, look for another stock that gives you an entry signal. Every day there are dozens of stocks that give you an entry signal. Only take the FIRST signal in a trend, then buy $0.01 above the high of the first GREEN bar or sell $0.01 below the first RED bar.

Part 3: When to Exit a Trade

Now that you know when to ENTER a trade, let's talk about when to EXIT a trade. The reality is that anyone can ENTER the market, but that's not where the money is made—or lost. Wealth happens—or takes a hit—when you EXIT the markets.

Let me say this again because it's important:

Money is made and lost when you EXIT the markets.

That's why knowing when to *exit* a trade is so important—arguably MORE important than knowing when to enter a trade. But, for some reason, too many traders get this wrong. They only focus on entries and don't worry about exits. And when they stay in the trade for too long, they're either hit with massive losses or leave money on the table.

Don't make that mistake!

I ALWAYS determine when to exit a trade even before I enter it. The end result? I can put the trade on autopilot and don't have to worry about it—easy.

Specifically, here are the three exit strategies I use:

1. A **Stop Loss** protects you from loss by limiting your risk
2. A **Profit Target** takes profit when the stock is moving in your favor
3. A **Black Bar Exit** gets you out of the market when it's moving sideways

Let's break each down a little more.

Exit 1: Stop Losses

A stop loss limits your risk by getting you out of a trade if it's moving against you. THIS is a key difference between profitable traders and unsuccessful traders.

Professional traders use stop losses and liquidate their positions with a small loss if the trade goes against them.

Unsuccessful traders do NOT use stop losses and, instead, simply hope the market turns around. This is a recipe for disaster.

Why?

Because often the market *doesn't* turn around which can turn small losses into large ones—I've seen these losses wipe out 20%, 30% or even 50% of a trader's accounts. I recently saw a trader with a losing position of more than $360,000. Yikes!

So the BIG question: what's the SMART way to place the limits on your losses?

Personally, I base my stop losses on the "Average Daily Range." To calculate it, simply subtract the low of the day from the high of the day and then take the average of the last seven days. In essence, we're calculating the price range (High to Low) on average for the past 7 trading days.

Average Daily Range (ADR) = Moving Average (High of Daily - Low of Daily for 7 days)

You can calculate this manually—I have my PowerX software calculate the **Average Daily Range** for me.

In the example below, the **Average Daily Range** is $0.42. For simplicity's sake, we're going to use $0.42 in the examples that follow to keep the math simple. In reality, that number would change slightly because it is always based on the prior 7 trading days when we're evaluating a trade.

For my stop loss, I like to use 1.5 times the Average Daily Range: **Stop Loss = Average Daily Range ***

*Please go to **PowerXStrategy.com/gift** to download the full-color chart companion guide to this book for FREE.*

In this example, my stop loss is $0.63 ($0.42 * 1.5).

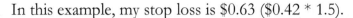

When we enter the trade at $8.36, we simply subtract $0.63 from our entry and place our stop loss at $7.73.

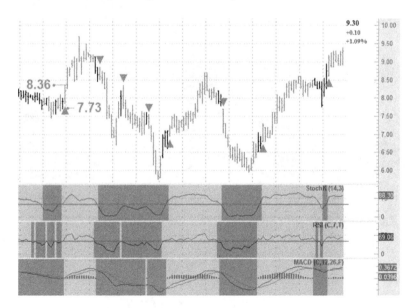

Here's another example. In this scenario, we enter the trade at $7.26 and simply subtract $0.63 from our entry and place our stop loss at $6.63.

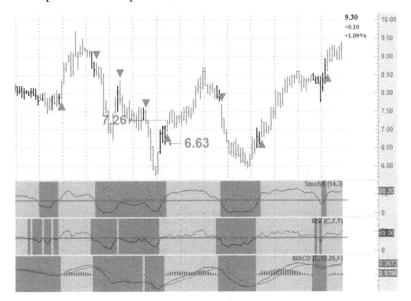

As you can see, the stop loss is perfect: If we enter at $7.26 and prices move down to $6.63, we know that we are wrong and exit immediately. This way we only risk $0.63 per share with a maximum loss of just $63 for 100 shares.

*Please go to **PowerXStrategy.com/gift** to download the full-color chart companion guide to this book for FREE.*

An Important Note Before Moving On:

Setting stop loss levels on shares of stock and orders to execute them through trading software is fairly clear-cut. It's a different situation when **options** are used on a PowerX Strategy trade. We still key off of the same stop-loss level that we calculated but we do not enter the exiting order to close out the options trade as we normally would with the stock.

When getting stopped out when using an option on the trade, we must watch the stock price closely and then manually initiate our stop loss exit of the trade based on the stock price falling below our calculated stop level.

We do this as to not get bad prices when exiting the options trade. Options markets can be wider than stock price markets and we may lose a good deal more than we bargained for if we key off of the option price itself to initiate our stop loss order.

Exit 2: Profit Target

Naturally, this is the most fun way to exit because we are taking a PROFIT. Here, there are two important things to remember:

#1: Nobody ever went broke taking profits

#2: There are only two ways to exit
—too early or too late!

I personally do not like to fixate on the market. **I want the market to come to my profit target levels that I've preset.** Having preset targets puts my mind at ease and allows the trades to play out without much emotion involved on my part.

As soon as I'm in a trade, I place my profit taking order so I don't have worry about the trade again. **If the stock moves in my favor, the order executes and sells the stock automatically as soon as it hits my profit target.**

By approaching matters this way, I do not need to watch every move the stock makes and I remove the emotions from my trading. I've found from working with the PowerX Strategy in many different market environments that it performs best when profit taking is directly related to potential losses by a 2 to 1 ratio with Average Daily Range as the base of the calculation.

For my profit target, I like to use three times the Average Daily Range (my PowerX software calculates this for me automatically):

Profit Target = Average Daily Range * 3

In this example, my profit target is $1.26 ($0.42 * 3).

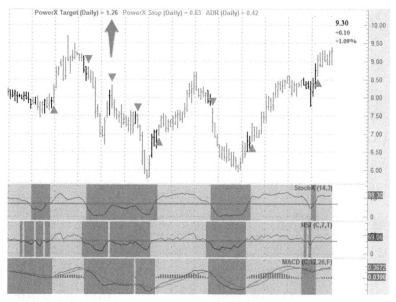

Before we dive into specific examples, here's a recap:

Our stop loss is 1.5 times the Average Daily Range = $0.63

And our profit target is three times the Average Daily Range = $1.26.

Since the profit target is twice as large as the stop loss, you can make money even if half of your trades are losing trades.

Please go to **PowerXStrategy.com/gift** *to download the full-color chart companion guide to this book for FREE.*

Think about that for a minute—it's extremely powerful. Let's say you're placing 10 trades with 100 shares each.

- Five of these trades are losing trades, so you lose 5 * $63 = $315
- Five of these trades are winning trades, so you make 5* $126 = $630

In this scenario, you have **$315 in profits** after 10 trades— even though HALF were losers.

Back to our previous example. We would enter the trade at $7.26, place our stop loss at $6.63 and place our profit target at $8.52 as shown below:

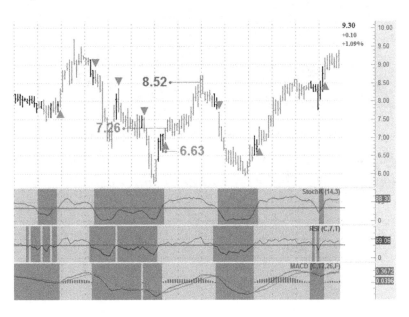

Here's another example:

- Entry is at $7.31
- Stop loss is placed at $6.68 ($7.31 - $0.63)
- Profit target is placed at $8.57 ($7.31 + $1.26)

As you can see, a few weeks after entering the trade, we hit our profit target—even though we NEVER came close to our stop loss. *That's the power of smart exits.*

Exit 3: Black Bar Exit

This exit is extremely powerful because **it enables you to exit a trade when the stock is going NOWHERE.**

Let's back up for a minute.

Any time you enter a trade, there are three possible scenarios:

1. **The stock will move *in your direction*.** This is, of course, great because you'll have a profit target in place.
2. **The stock could move *against you*.** In this case, you have your stop loss in place to help limit your losses.
3. **The stock goes *sideways*.** In this case, you need a rule to get out of the trade and free up your capital for the next trade. Because when a stock is going sideways, you're not making any money—not ideal.

In scenario three, you'll use the Black Bar Exit.

Let's break it down.

Understanding the Black Bar Exit

Remember that some charting software allows you to color the bars based on the criteria of the PowerX Strategy. The chart shows GREEN bars when all three indicators are signaling an UPTREND. And, when indicators are signaling a DOWNTREND, you'll see RED bars. When there's NO trend—i.e. the indicators are giving conflicting signals—the market is moving *sideways*. In these scenarios, you'll see BLACK BARS.

When that happens, it's important to close the trade at open, the day after the black bar occurred.

Here's an example:

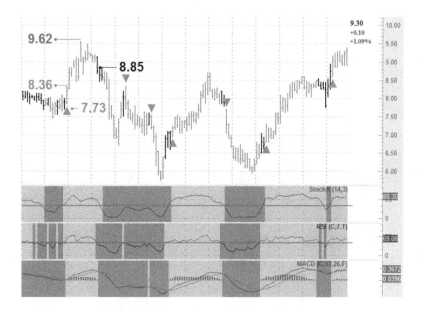

- The entry is at $8.36
- The stop loss is at $7.73 ($8.36 - $0.63)
- The profit target is at $9.62 ($8.36 + $1.26)

The price never hit the profit target of $9.62. In this case, the stock moved up to $9.55 and then it turned around. If we ONLY had a profit target and a stop loss, we would get stopped out with a loss rather than taking profits at this point.

A few days after the stock tops out at $9.55, though, we see a black bar. We place an order to exit the trade at the open following the day on which we saw the black bar, and exit the trade at $8.85.

Let's review why this exit strategy is so important in this example:

- Without the Black Bar Exit, we would have been stopped out at $7.73 **for a loss of $0.63 per share** or $63 for 100 shares.
- With the Black Bar Exit, we exit the trade at $8.85 **for a profit of $0.49 per share** or $49 for 100 shares. That's a 6% gain for the short time we were in the trade.

If you want to make it as a trader, it's essential you ALWAYS apply ALL THREE exit strategies:

1. Stop Loss
2. Profit Target
3. Black Bar Exit

An Important Note Before Moving On:

You may have noticed that many of the examples of the PowerX Strategy in action were based on lower priced stocks. The reason for this is simple:

It's much easier for lower priced stocks to make LARGER PERCENTAGE moves than higher priced stocks.

As this is the case, our trades can be efficient in terms of holding time. We're not tied up for very long waiting for bigger percentage moves that generally take longer to transpire in higher priced stocks. However, a good trade is a good trade and we'll take them as they come in stocks at various prices across the price spectrum.

CHAPTER 4

Leverage Your Account with Options

WHY trade options? It's a BIG, IMPORTANT question, especially if you aren't yet trading options…

YET.

There are countless benefits to trading options, including:

- **You can use your existing accounts:** You can trade options in most brokerage accounts and even some retirement accounts. That means there's no need to open new accounts.

- **Options are perfect for small accounts:** You don't need a lot of money to trade options. You will learn a way to trade options for as little as $100 per contract.

- **Start small, but grow BIG:** You can start with as little as $2,000 in your account and use options to potentially grow your account to $20,000, $50,000 or even more!

- **Limited risk:** You already know that you must limit your risk. The best thing about options? Done right you'll rarely lose more than you invest!

- **Leverage:** Options allow you to control shares of stock for a fraction of the price of buying the actual shares but you get the full benefit of the price movement when the stock moves in your favor.

Scratching your head yet? I get it. *If options are so fantastic, why isn't EVERYONE trading options?*

The short answer? There are a few myths about trading options swirling around the market, which deters some traders from diving in. The reality is, most AREN'T true— not even a little. So let's take a minute and dispel those myths...

Myth #1. "It's complicated!"

Many traders make trading options more complicated than it has to be. They focus on "Spreads", "The Greeks" and other details. As you'll quickly see, trading options can be straightforward. My goal is to show you a simple way to dig into—and make money from—options.

Myth #2. "Most options expire worthless, so you shouldn't buy options."

For many stocks, hundreds of options exist. Many of them are effectively longshot bets with little chance of success!! As an example, there are options that will ONLY make money if the stock price jumps 50% in the next few days. Is that possible? Sure. Everything is possible in the markets. Is it likely to happen? NO! And that's why options like this expire worthless. And there are a LOT of worthless options trades in the market due to traders who don't know what they are doing. Unlike them, you are getting educated on options right now.

Think about it like an insurance policy. There are many insurance options out there that make sense—think home and car, for starters. Then, there are a few that make NO sense. Right now in the U.S., more than 20,000 people are paying for an insurance against "alien abduction, alien impregnation and consumption by aliens." Think about THAT for a minute. How likely are you to EVER need that insurance? Exactly—NEVER!

Options are the same. Learn how to trade the "right" options—the options that will actually KEEP their value—and you'll make profits.

Myth #3. "You have to be good at math..."

Being good at math isn't required to use options effectively. Some traders like to make options sound overly complicated but they can be used in a simple fashion but produce great results.

The truth? *Once you master simplicity, you earn complexity.* I'll show you a simple way to get started with options so you can start trading options with a simple and effective trading strategy. You'll learn to walk before you run and position yourself for success with options.

An Important Note Before Moving On:

The PowerX system allows for traders to use whatever is best suited for them, at their discretion, be it shares of stock or options contracts. Many factors to consider when deciding on which is the best fit will be unique to each trader. Account size and level of experience will be two of the most critical factors along with the price of the stock under consideration for a trade. The liquidity of the options markets and the liquidity in the stock itself should also play a role in determining which is the most suitable investment vehicle for that particular trade.

Option Trading 101

If you're brand new to options, this section is for you. And if you've traded options before—even successfully— STILL READ THIS SECTION. It's always good to get back to basics with something so important.

Let's start with an example. You want to buy a house for $200,000 but you don't have that much money. You need to "leverage" the bank's money they loan to you to complete the home purchase. To kick off the process, you'll need to bring some money to the table—a down payment, specifically. The amount of your down payment depends on many factors. For the sake of simplicity, let's say you're going to put 5% down—$10,000.

Now let's assume the house appreciates to $220,000 *after* you close. How much money did you make from this purchase?

Did you say 10%?

It's simple, right? The value of the house increased by $20,000 or, in this case, 10%.

If you said 10%, you'd be in the majority. *And you'd be* WRONG.

The right answer? 200%.

Think about it. The bank gave you $190,000. If you were to sell the house right now, you'd have to pay the bank $190,000 back, leaving you with $30,000 in cash. Of that $30,000, $10,000 was your initial down payment. Subtract that out and you're left with a $20,000 profit —on the $10,000 you invested.

Making sense?

So even though the underlying asset—the house— only appreciated by 10%, you would be able to make 200% based on the money you brought to the deal.

That's exactly how options work.

What is an Option?

An option gives the buyer the <u>right, but not the obligation,</u> to <u>buy or sell the underlying stock</u> at a <u>certain price</u>—AKA a "strike" price—before a <u>pre-defined date</u>, also known as the *expiration date*.

There are two types of options:

- A **CALL** gives you the right to **BUY** the underlying stock at a certain price (strike price) before a pre-defined date (expiration date)
- A **PUT** gives you the right to **SELL** the underlying stock at a certain price (strike price) before a pre-defined date (expiration date)

It's important to note that the option is a "right" and not an "obligation." As a BUYER of an option, you CAN buy the underlying stock at a certain price—a strike price—before a pre-defined expiration date, but you don't have to.

That may seem minor, but it's a very important designation. Soon, you'll see why.

Understanding Strike Prices

The strike price specifies the price at which you can buy or sell the underlying stock. The strike prices are predefined by the option exchanges.

Let's say, for example, a stock is trading at $10.00. The pre-defined strike prices for the option are $9, $10, $12.50, $15.00 and so on.

- If you buy a CALL with a strike price of $9.00, you have the right—but not the obligation—to BUY the stock for $9.00. Since the price of the stock is currently at $10.00, this option has an "intrinsic" value of $1.00. Why?

- o Because you COULD buy the option with a strike price of $9.00
- o THEN immediately exercise your right to buy the stock for $9.00
- o THEN sell it for $10.00 in the market, since THAT is the current market value

Therefore, the option will be worth at least $1.00. This is called the "intrinsic value."

In addition to the INTRINSIC value, options also have EXTRINSIC value. On a call, the EXTRINSIC VALUE is based on the probability that the stock price will be above the option's strike price at or before the expiration date.

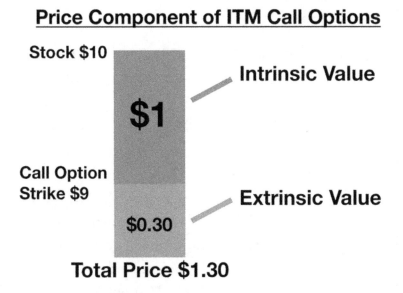

Price Component of ITM Call Options

If you're confused right now, hang in there—the worst is over! And if you understood THIS concept, you (almost) know what you need to know to roll up your sleeves and dive in.

Let's take a look at another stock with a different strike price. In this second example, the stock is trading at $11.00 and you own the CALL option with a strike price of $12.50. This means that you have the right to BUY the underlying stock before the expiration date for $12.50.

Clearly, the option doesn't have any INTRINSIC VALUE right now—only if the stock moves above $12.50. But let's say that happens. Let's say the stock moves from $11.00 to $13.00. In this case, the $12.50 option would now have an INTRINSIC value of $0.50.

Some other important details to keep in mind about options and their value:

- If the strike price of a CALL option is BELOW the current value of the stock—in other words, if the option price has INTRINSIC value—the option is called "in-the-money" (ITM). In our first example above, the stock price was at $10.00, the $9.00 strike option would be an ITM option.
- If the strike price of a CALL option is ABOVE the current value of the stock—the option price has <u>NO</u> INTRINSIC value—the option is called "out-of-the-money" (OTM). In our second example, the $12.50 option would be an OTM option.

- If the strike price of a CALL option is the *same* as the current value of the stock, the option would be called "at-the-money" (ATM). In our first example, a $10.00 strike option would be an ATM option.

Understanding Expiration Dates

Another key detail of options is their expiration dates. Every option has an "expiration date." Once the option expires, you no longer have the right to buy (or sell) the underlying stock for the strike price.

At the expiration date, the value of an option is the same as the INTRINSIC value.

- If your option is "in-the-money," (ITM) then the option still has some value.
- "At the money" (ATM) and "out-of-the-money" (OTM) options don't have any value when the clock strikes zero.
- The extrinsic value gets smaller every day. This is called "time decay."
- The closer an option gets to expiration, the quicker the EXTRINSIC value disappears.

Think of it like a snowman in the sun. In the beginning, the option loses a little bit of extrinsic value, just like a snowman melts slower in the beginning. But, as we get closer to the expiration date, the option loses more and more value, just like the snowman melts faster and faster.

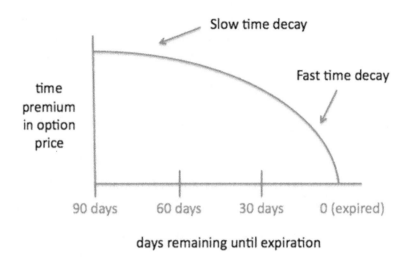

days remaining until expiration

As you can see, it's important to pick an expiration date that gives you enough time before expiration. However, options with a long time until expiration are also more expensive.

In my experience, the sweet spot is 30-45 days until expiration. This time frame provides us with an adequate amount of time for the trade to transpire but helps us to avoid the extrinsic value portion of the option's rapid loss phase. **In other words, although the "sweet spot" for holding trades with the PowerX system is 10 to 20 days, we buy our options further out in time (30-45 days) so that we avoid the very rapid loss of extrinsic value** that options suffer in the final 3 weeks prior to their expiration. Referencing the Decay Curve above, note the rapid loss of value at the very end phase of the option's life.

Size of an Option Contract

IMPORTANT: Options control shares of stock!

You can NOT buy an option on a single share of stock. **When you buy an option contract, you actually buy the right to buy or sell 100 shares of stock.**

This is important!

Option prices are stated on a "per share" basis so that their quotes are consistent with stock price quotes which are also quoted on a per share basis. Each standardized options contract is for 100 shares of stock. So, this is how it all works out. If the price of the option is $2.00 in the markets and you want to buy one option contract, you'll actually have to pay $200 in the real world ($2.00 per share * 100) shares that the contract controls.

Why?

It has to do with "round lots". Any trade of stock that is not an even number of shares in blocks of 100 is considered an "odd lot". Round lots are trades that take place that are in hundreds or thousands. Most trades are round lots and thus are traded in blocks of hundreds, thousands or tens of thousands. Option contracts were set to control 100 shares as round lots are what most people and institutions tend to prefer to execute. **100 shares thus became the standard sized equity (stock options contract).**

Options Strategies

There are many options trading strategies that options traders will use based on the underlying stock, the opportunity they see, their personal risk tolerance, knowledge and experience, goals, etc. This quick reference guide provides a long list of options strategies from pretty simple to complex.

Option Strategy Quick Reference Guide

Strategy	Risk Profile	Strategy	Market Outlook	Profit Potential	Risk Potential	Time Decay Effect
Long Call		B1 - C	Bullish	Unlimited	Limited	Detrimental
Short Call		S1 - C	Bearish	Limited	Unlimited	Helpful
Long Put		B1 - P	Bearish	Unlimited	Limited	Detrimental
Short Put		S1 - P	Bullish	Limited	Unlimited	Helpful
Bull Call Spread		B1 - LC / S1 - HC	Moderately Bullish	Limited	Limited	Mixed
Bull Put Spread		B1 - LP / S1 - HP	Moderately Bullish	Limited	Limited	Mixed
Bear Put Spread		B1 - HP / S1 - LP	Moderately Bearish	Limited	Limited	Mixed
Bear Call Spread		B1 - HC / S1 - LC	Moderately Bearish	Limited	Limited	Mixed
Long Straddle		B1 - ATM - C / B1 - ATM - P	Volatile	Unlimited	Limited	Detrimental
Short Straddle		S1 - ATM - C / S1 - ATM - P	Stable	Limited	Unlimited	Helpful
Long Strangle		B1 - OTM - C / B1 - OTM - P	Volatile	Unlimited	Limited	Detrimental
Short Strangle		S1 - OTM - C / S1 - OTM - P	Stable	Limited	Unlimited	Helpful
Call Ratio Back Spread		S1 - LC / B2 - HC	Strongly Bullish	Unlimited	Limited	Mixed
Put Ratio Back Spread		S1 - HP / B2 - LP	Strongly Bearish	Unlimited	Limited	Mixed
Long Butterfly		B1-LC S2-HC S1-HC / B1-LP S2-HP S1-HP	Stable	Limited	Limited	Helpful
Short Butterfly		S1-LC B2-HC S1-HC / S1-LP B2-HP S1-HP	Bullish or Bearish	Limited	Limited	Detrimental
Long Condor		B1-LC S1-HC S1-HC B1-HC / B1-LP S1-HP S1-HP B1-HP	Stable	Limited	Limited	Helpful
Short Condor		S1-LC B1-HC B1-HC S1-HC / S1-LP B1-HP B1-HP S1-HP	Bullish or Bearish	Limited	Limited	Detrimental
Long Iron Butterfly		S1-ATM-C, B1-OTM-C / S1-ATM-P, B1-OTM-P	Stable	Limited	Limited	Helpful
Short Iron Butterfly		B1-ATM-C, S1-OTM-C / B1-ATM-P, S1-OTM-P	Bullish or Bearish	Limited	Limited	Detrimental
Call Calendar		B1-LC, longer term / S1-HC, shorter term	Moderately Bullish	Limited	Limited	Mixed
Put Calendar		B1-HP, longer term / S1-LP, shorter term	Moderately Bearish	Limited	Limited	Mixed
Inverted Diag Iron Butterfly		B1-LC-LT, S1-HC-ST / B1-HP-LT, S1-LP-ST	Range Bound or Stable	Limited	Limited	Mixed

As you can see, options traders like to use interesting names for their trading strategies like "Condor," "Butterfly," "Spread," "Straddle" and "Strangle."

So which of these options trading strategies are the best?

It depends. On a LOT of factors.

FOR NOW, my advice is simple—*KEEP IT SIMPLE.*

- When you want to BUY a stock, buy a CALL
- When you want to SELL a stock, buy a PUT

If you can't make money with these simple strategies, it's very unlikely you will make money with more complex strategies. Try these first, and then you can move on to "Spreads," "Condors," and

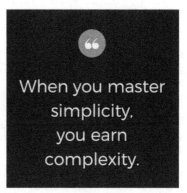

When you master simplicity, you earn complexity.

other more advanced options strategies. But for now, make THESE approaches your go-tos to master.

An Options Trade Example

Let's run through a quick example to bring everything together. Below is a stock that gave us an entry signal to BUY for $11.10. Based on the calculations that I gave you in the previous chapter, we place our stop loss at $10.59 and our profit target at $12.12. Remember, we arrived at the stop loss of $10.59 by way of our ADR (Average Daily Range) and stop loss calculations covered earlier. The ADR in the example below is $0.34 and if we multiply that by 1.5 we come to $0.51 which we subtract from our $11.10 buy level to produce $10.59 which is our stop level. My PowerX software does these calculations for me automatically based on my account size.

As you can see, a few days after entering the trade, the profit target was hit, and we made $1.02 per share or $102 for 100 shares. **That's 9% profit in just a few days!**

Not bad at all, is it?

But let's take a look at a possible option trade.

On the day the stock traded above the high of the previous day and we entered the stock at $11.10, the CALL option with a strike price of $10.00 and 45 days to expiration was trading at $1.20.

A few days later, when the stock hit the profit target, the option was trading at $2.22.

That's 85% profit in just a few days on the options trade!

Let's compare the results of the stock trade to the option trade:

	Buy 100 Shares of Stock	Buy 1 Option Contract (Controls 100 Shares)
Investment needed	$1,110	$120
Profit	$102	$102
Profit in %	9%	85%

Trading options is starting to sound pretty exciting, isn't it? That's why, next up, we'll unpack the PowerX Strategy and show you how you can use it to trade options.

CHAPTER 5

Trading Options with the PowerX Strategy

Every option is tied to an underlying stock. Therefore, before we can make a move, we need to look at the stock and decide whether it's going up, down or sideways. To do that, we'll leverage the PowerX Strategy to determine when to buy a stock—the exact process outlined earlier in this book.

Selecting the Best Option

Let's start with an example. In this chart, all three indicators are signaling BUY. And today, the price of the stock moved above the high of the "signal bar". If we want to trade the stock, we would BUY the stock at $13.96. Based on the stop loss and profit target calculations that you learned in the last chapter, the stop loss for this trade would be at \$13.27 and the profit target is at \$15.34.

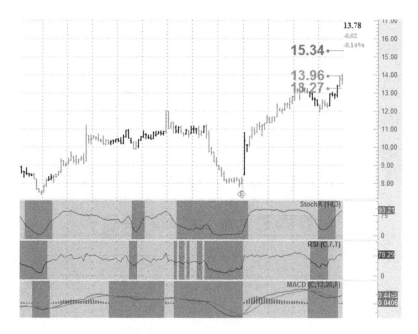

Instead of trading the stock, we're going to trade OPTIONS this time. *However, we still have to look at the stock to see what it's doing, since the option is tied to the stock.*

The stock gave us an entry signal, so we can now look for an option. Earlier, we talked about "in-the-money," "at-the-money" and "out-of-the-money" options. So here are those three choices:

Option	DTE	Strike	Call/Put	Entry Price
ITM (conservative)	40	12.5	CALL	1.99
ATM (medium aggressive)	40	15	CALL	0.75
OTM (aggressive)	40	17.5	CALL	0.23

*Please go to **PowerXStrategy.com/gift** to download the full-color chart companion guide to this book for FREE.*

All three options have 40 days to expiration (DTE), which is plenty of time. And since we want to BUY the stock, we are looking at CALL options.

- The "In-The-Money (ITM)" option has a strike price of $12.50 and costs $1.99 = $199 per option contract.
- The "At-The-Money (ITM)" option has a strike price of $15.00 and costs $0.75 = $75 per option contract.
- The "Out-Of-The-Money (ITM)" option has a strike price of $17.50 and costs $0.23 = $23 per option contract.

Of course, we don't make our decision just based on the price. The OTM option is a long-shot, and might not be worth anything when we reach our profit target. Therefore, **I personally don't trade "out-of-the-money" options. My preferred types of options are "in-the-money"** since they hold their value very well and move very similar to the stock price.

But let's compare these three options so you can see what it all looks like. My PowerX software automatically calculates for me how much the option should be worth when the stock reaches the profit target and the stop loss.

When trading, you always want to make conservative estimations. It's always better to be positively surprised!

Based on my calculations:

Option	DTE	Strike	Call/Put	Entry Price	Option at Target	Option at Stop
ITM (conservative)	40	12.5	CALL	1.99	2.95	1.42
ATM (medium aggressive)	40	15	CALL	0.75	1.27	0.42
OTM (aggressive)	40	17.5	CALL	0.23	0.40	0.09

- The "in-the-money" (ITM) option should be worth $2.95 when the stock reaches the profit target. Therefore, my potential profit for this option is $0.96. Based on the entry price of $1.99, that's a profit of 48%.
- The "at-the-money" (ATM) option should be worth $1.27 when the stock reaches the profit target. Therefore, my potential profit for this option is $0.52. Based on the entry price of $0.75, that's a profit of 69%.
- The "out-of-the-money" (OTM) option should be worth $0.40 when the stock reaches the profit target. Therefore, my potential profit for this option is $0.17. Based on the entry price of $0.23, that's a profit of 74%.

But that's still not all. Before you make a decision, it's important to look at the risk associated with a trade.

- The "ITM" option should still be worth $1.42 when the stock reaches the stop loss. Therefore, my potential risk for this option is $0.57. Based on the profit potential of $0.96, the risk/reward ratio would be 1:1.7. Which means, we'd be risking $0.57 to make $0.95 on this trade when using the option.
- The "ATM" option should still be worth $0.42 when the stock reaches the stop loss. Therefore, my

potential risk for this option is $0.33. Based on the profit potential of $0.52, the risk/reward ratio would be 1:1.6. Which means, we'd be risking $0.33 to make $0.52 on this trade when using the option.

- The "OTM" option should still be worth $0.09 when the stock reaches the stop loss. Therefore, my potential risk for this option is $0.14. Based on the profit potential of $0.17, the risk/reward ratio would be 1:1.2. Which means, we'd be risking $0.14 to make $0.17 on this trade when using the option.

As you can see, the risk/reward ratio is best when trading the "ITM" option. For every $1 that we risk, we can expect to make at least $1.70—and that's why "ITM" options are my favorite type of option.

You may have noticed that the ratios of the ITM and ATM are fairly close, and of course, you can choose any of these options you want, **but my default is the "ITM" option as general rule.**

When to Enter the Options Trade

Once you decide which option you want to trade, it's time to enter the option trade into your brokerage platform. Just keep in mind that **FIRST, the stock price must move above the high of the signal bar BEFORE entering the options trade** (all three technical indicators we use align creating a "BUY" signal).

When to Exit the Options Trade

Since every option is tied to an underlying stock you must watch the stock for exit signals. **As soon as the stock gives you a signal to exit, you must exit the option.**

Just like I showed you in stocks, there are three types of exits:

1. Stop Loss
2. Profit Target
3. Black Bar

After entering an options trade, take a quick look after the markets close to see if the stock gives an exit signal.

In this example, the stock is moving up as expected after a few days—but we haven't reached our profit target yet.

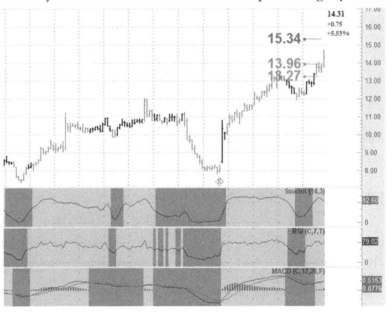

*Please go to **PowerXStrategy.com/gift** to download the full-color chart companion guide to this book for FREE.*

In this case, you'd keep monitoring the stock. As soon as either the profit target or the stop loss is hit—or you wind up with a black bar—you need to exit the options trade to take your profits or limit your risk. When you think about it all that way, it's very simple, isn't it?

Now you know the strategy that I use in my trading daily, you know how to pick the stock or option and enter and exit the trades, **but even if you have the best strategy in the world, you can still lose money if you do not have the proper money management.**

In the next chapter I will **share the money management system that not only saved my account, it potentially allows you to turn $5000 into $41,400 in only 12 months.** Let's dig in...

CHAPTER 6

How to Grow a Small Account into a Bigger One

Money management is a huge piece of the trading conversation—but, amazingly, it's often overlooked completely. *If you want to grow your small trading account into a large account, you need to employ rock-solid money management strategies from the beginning.* If you really understand and harness the power of effective money management, you'll be able to grow your account even without actually improving the performance of your trades.

Money Management 101

What's the biggest lesson I can teach you at this point? You won't necessarily be profitable on day one. Your trading business will grow over time and you want to plan for that. The best way? By being consistent and ensuring you aren't trading too aggressively, especially in the beginning. If you do, you're going to get wiped out. And if you run too far in the other direction, if you go SUPER conservative with your trading, that's no good either. No one wants to be a one-lot trader for the rest of their life. Eventually, you need to spread your wings and trade more shares or contracts. It's important to keep in mind that you still need to respect how much you're putting into any one trade. As a general rule, I rarely put any more than 5% of my trading account funds in any one trade.

This is, hands down, one of the biggest pitfalls for new and experienced traders. People get impatient—they aren't making enough money in their mind and they start trading at a crazy, aggressive clip. I did it early on—I'm not afraid to admit it. I thought I should be making more money and so I put my head down and started trading like there was no tomorrow. The end result? There almost wasn't—for me and my trading business, at least. Because the markets just HAMMERED me.

Fast forward 15 years and I realize my experience is far from the exception—it's the rule. **If you try to come at the market too aggressively, it's going to punish you.** As traders, we need to **focus on consistency and clarity**. Start small, prove you can be consistently profitable and, from there, apply the principles of money management to grow your trading account—and your WEALTH—even more.

Understanding Money Management

So, let's take a step back because understanding money management as it relates to trading and risk is critical to success as a trader.

Simply, money management refers to a systematic approach to grow your account.

Your Money Management Plan will tell you exactly how much money you should risk based on your account size to optimally grow your account.

While every trader will, ultimately, come up with their own rules when it comes to money management, here are two key concepts that I like to apply:

1. *If you are profitable, you can increase your risk per trade.*

   Earlier I said that I rarely put any more than 5% of my trading account funds in any one trade. That amount is when I'm very confident and have a good track record with my strategy. In the beginning, I follow a 2% rule: "Never risk more than 2% of your account on any given trade." And that's a great rule to live by until you have proven your trading.

   However, once you have a good track record, in order to grow your account, you have to violate the 2% rule, and here's why:

Trading is a function of risk and reward.

We've already talked about my Golden Rule: 1 to 2 - you are trying to make $2 for every $1 that you risk. Or $20 for every $10 you risk. Remember, this is critical because even if you only win 50% of the time you'll still come out ahead. You know the basic concept.

So, the more you risk, the higher the reward in dollar terms:

- If you risk $200 on a trade, you are trying to make $400.
- If you risk $400 on a trade, you are trying to make $800.

My rule of thumb is that you should only risk more if you have proven to yourself that you can make money for at least 4 weeks in a row. In a moment I will give you more specifics on that, but first let's talk about the second important concept:

2. *When you lose money, you need to reduce your risk per trade.*

As long as you are making money, you are allowed to increase your risk - and therefore, your profits. But when you lose money, you have to reduce your risk per trade. This approach is called an "anti-martingale approach", and it's the best way to grow your account safely.

Why Money Management Matters

Larry Williams is a trader who became famous for winning the World Cup Futures Trading Championship by turning a $10,000 account to $1,100,000 in 12 months.

He was asked, how he was able to achieve such an amazing growth in his account.

Here's what he said:

"For years people have asked for my trades to figure out how I did it. I gladly oblige them, they will learn that – what created the gargantuan gain was not great trading ability barely as much as **the very aggressive form of money management I used** . The approach was to buy more contracts when I had more equity in my account, cut back when I had less."

Here's another reason why Money Management is so important:

Even Geniuses *with a Profitable Strategy* Can Lose In Trading: The Ralph Vince Experiment

Ralph Vince is a well-respected and well-known financial investor and educator. He's published a number of books on trading and the trading industry, and he also performed a very famous experiment known as the Ralph Vince Experiment.

Mr. Vince took 40 Ph.D.'s and set them up to trade with a computer game.

All 40 people had doctoral degrees, but Mr. Vince made sure that none of their degrees involved any sort of background in statistics or trading.

In the game, each of them were given $1,000 and 100 trades, with a 60% winning percentage.

When they won, they won the amount of money they risked.

When they lost, they lost the amount of money they risked.

Simple.

In this experiment, ALL of them had a profitable trading strategy, because 60 of their 100 trades were winning trades. If they risked $10 on every trade, they would have won $600 (60 * $10) and lost $400 (40 * $10). So, after 100 trades, they would have made $200.

Easy enough, isn't it?

But in this experiment, after all 40 PhDs had completed their 100 trades, how many do you think made money? **2.**

Only 2 out of 40 were able to make money. The other 38 failed to succeed.

95% of these "smart" people lost money, because of what came down to being poor Money Management!

(Source: CSI News Journal, March 1992)

Here's what happens when people begin to fail at a few trades... they begin to reason that they're overdue for a winner or a big score. In other words, their *"gambler mentality"* kicks in. They want to get out of the hole they're in fast and get back to even. They abandon their discipline. They leave behind key parts of their money management system. They even begin to get sloppy with what was formerly a reliable strategy. These human tendencies are what we must manage to be consistently successful in the trading markets.

As you can see, Money Management is extremely important for ANY account size, and it is critical if you want to grow a small account and turn it into a bigger one.

The Best Money Management Approach

There are many money management approaches. Here are just a few:

- *Percent Risk*
  This is the typical "2% Rule." You risk no more than 2% of your account on any given trade. As your account grows, you may decide to risk more. And although this is a great low-risk money management strategy, that we use when are are starting out, it won't help you to grow your account quickly.

- *Optimal F*
  The Optimal F system of money management was devised by Ralph Vince, and he's written several books about this and other money management topics. The idea is that you determine the ideal

fraction of your money to allocate per trade based on past performance. If your Optimal F is 18%, then each trade should be 18 percent of your account — no more, no less. And although this is a good advanced money management strategy, it requires complicated calculations. PLUS: You must have the detailed performance of your strategy, and very few traders have the key performance metrics that are required for this money management approach to be utilized.

- *Fixed Ratio*
  This is my personal favorite, since it's easy to follow and allows you to grow your account quickly. Here's how the Fixed Ratio works:

Let's assume you start with a $10,000 account on Feb 1st, 2018.

When you start trading, you apply the 2% Rule, i.e. you risk no more than 2% of your account on one trade. 2% of $10,000 is $200.

The table below shows the suggested risk:

Your Long-Term Plan									

| Starting Equity | $ 10,000.00 |
| Start Date | 2/1/18 |

| $ Goal/week | $ 100.00 per trade |

| Trading Days to next level | 20 |
| Trading Weeks to next level | 4 |

Date at next level	From	To	Risk/Trade	Total Risk	Weekly Profit		Min Equity	Dip
1-Feb-18	10000	10399	200	1000	$ 100.00		9000	10%
1-Mar-18	10400	11199	400	2000	200.00		8400	19%
29-Mar-18	11200	12399	600	3000	300.00		8200	27%

If you apply my Golden Rule, when you risk $200 you are trying to make $400.

You will have some losing trades, and you will have some winning trades. Your goal is to make $100 per week on a $10,000 account.

Do you believe that THIS is a realistic goal? Of course it is!

So, if you make $100 per week, you will make $400 within 4 weeks and your account grows from $10,000 to $10,400.

And that's when the magic happens.

If you were able to make $100 per week <u>consistently</u> for 4 weeks in a row, you have now earned the right to risk more and may now risk $400 on every trade:

Your Long-Term Plan							

Starting Equity $ 10,000.00
Start Date 2/1/18

$ Goal/week $ 100.00 per trade

Trading Days to next level 20
Trading Weeks to next level 4

Date at next level	From	To	Risk/Trade	Total Risk	Weekly Profit	Min Equity	Dip
1-Feb-18	10000	10399	200	1000	$ 100.00	9000	10%
1-Mar-18	10400	11199	400	2000	200.00	8400	19%
29-Mar-18	11200	12399	600	3000	300.00	8200	27%

And since you are now risking $400, you are trying to make $800 per trade.

Let's recap:

- You have proven to yourself that you can make $100 per week <u>consistently</u> for 4 weeks.
- You now allow yourself to increase your risk from $200 to $400 per trade.
- Therefore, your profit goal automatically increases from $400 to $800.
- With your increased risk and profit goal, you are now trying to make **$200 per week** instead of $100 per week.

Making sense?

If you achieve your goal of making $200 per week <u>consistently</u> for the next 4 weeks, your account will grow by $800 from $10,400 to $11,200.

The first 4 weeks you're growing your account from $10,000 to $10,400.

And the next 4 weeks you're growing your account from $10,400 to $11,200.

And since you started on Feb 1st, 2018, your account should theoretically be at $11,200 on March 29th, 2018.

Now you may decide to increase your risk again from $400 to $600 per trade.

Would you like to plug in your own equity figures in and see how it would play out for you? Go to **PowerXStrategy.com/gift** for your own spreadsheet.

This table shows the potential progression of your increased risk, profit goals and account growth:

Your Long-Term Plan							

Starting Equity	$ 10,000.00						
Start Date	2/1/18						

$ Goal/week	$ 100.00 per trade						

Trading Days to next level	20						
Trading Weeks to next level	4						

Date at next level	From	To	Risk/Trade	Total Risk	Weekly Profit	Min Equity	Dip
1-Feb-18	10000	10399	200	1000	$ 100.00	9000	10%
1-Mar-18	10400	11199	400	2000	200.00	8400	19%
29-Mar-18	11200	12399	600	3000	300.00	8200	27%

Since you are now risking $600 per trade and you apply the "Golden Rule", your profit goal is now $1,200. Therefore, you no longer try to make $200 per week, you are now trying to make $300 per week.

And after you prove to yourself that you can make $300 per week for the next 4 weeks, your account will grow by $1,200 (4 weeks * $300).

So, your account grows from $11,200 to $12,400 by April 26, 2018.

As soon as there's more than $12,400 in your account, you are allowed to increase your risk again from $600 to $800.

And you increase your profit goal from $1,200 to $1,600 since you are applying the "Golden Rule:" You risk $800 and try to make $1,600.

The table below shows exactly when you should increase your risk, and therefore, your profit goal:

Date at next level	From	To	Risk/Trade	Total Risk	Weekly Profit	Min Equity	Dip
1-Feb-18	10000	10399	200	1000	$ 100.00	9000	10%
1-Mar-18	10400	11199	400	2000	200.00	8400	19%
29-Mar-18	11200	12399	600	3000	300.00	8200	27%
26-Apr-18	12400	13999	800	4000	400.00	8400	32%
24-May-18	14000	15999	1000	5000	500.00	9000	36%
21-Jun-18	16000	18399	1200	6000	600.00	10000	38%
19-Jul-18	18400	21199	1400	7000	700.00	11400	38%
16-Aug-18	21200	24399	1600	8000	800.00	13200	38%
13-Sep-18	24400	27999	1800	9000	900.00	15400	37%
11-Oct-18	28000	31999	2000	10000	1,000.00	18000	36%
8-Nov-18	32000	36399	2200	11000	1,100.00	21000	34%
6-Dec-18	36400	41199	2400	12000	1,200.00	24400	33%
3-Jan-19	41200	46399	2600	13000	1,300.00	28200	32%
31-Jan-19	46400	51999	2800	14000	1,400.00	32400	30%
28-Feb-19	52000	57999	3000	15000	1,500.00	37000	29%
28-Mar-19	58000	64399	3200	16000	1,600.00	42000	28%
25-Apr-19	64400	71199	3400	17000	1,700.00	47400	26%
23-May-19	71200	78399	3600	18000	1,800.00	53200	25%
20-Jun-19	78400	85999	3800	19000	1,900.00	59400	24%

As you can see, after 1 year of trading, you could potentially grow a $10,000 into $52,000 by Feb 28, 2019!!!

And within 18 months, you could grow your account to $86,000!

THAT is the power of Money Management!

The right Money Management approach is like a turbo-boost for your account!

7

Trading Pitfalls... and How to AVOID THEM

Sometimes bad things happen—I'll just say it. Sometimes, no matter how solid your system or how much you prepare or how robust your foundation is, things don't go right. *As a trader, one of the best qualities you can display is resiliency*—that you can pick yourself up, brush yourself off and keep moving forward, even after a rough day of trading or a lengthy loss period.

Simply laughing off the losses isn't a good strategy either. But trading is a game of ups and downs and twists and turns. If you can't stomach them, then you probably aren't going to last all that long—and you definitely aren't going to see the kinds of profits I'm talking about.

That said, while some challenges are unavoidable, there are plenty you can steer clear of from the beginning. In my 20-plus years as a trader, I've seen 10 major pitfalls that seem to rear their ugly heads over and over again. It doesn't matter if I'm dealing with novice traders or experienced pros. These mistakes seem to follow everyone everywhere they go—until you take the reins, take back the power and say NO MORE.

That's what I want to cover in this chapter.

Because, in the spirit of total transparency, I'll admit I've made every single one of these mistakes—and I've made them more than a few times. That's how I learned. But you don't have to learn by doing—and failing. *You can learn from my lifetime of mistakes, missteps and misunderstandings.* The upside? It's cheaper, easier and won't be nearly as discouraging than falling down the rabbit hole of these all too common trading pitfalls.

MISTAKE #1:
Treating Your Simulator Like a Game

If you're new to trading, I'm all for you using a simulator. You'll have an opportunity to try your hand at trading without investing real money. This will help you get used to trends, market shifts and - most importantly - the PowerX Strategy.

But that's where it should end.

Testing on a simulator serves two distinct purposes:

1. Testing a strategy and
2. Getting practice with your plan

And here's what you should NOT do on a simulator: Trade "crazy stuff", i.e. going crazy and "betting everything on red" or anything that has nothing to do with your plan!

The problem is that simulators are easy to reset and, let's be honest, they mean *nothing* at the end of the day. Start coloring outside the lines, and you can easily fool yourself into believing you're some kind of superstar trader, even if you're new to the industry.

I see it happen all the time. Someone starts up a $100,000 simulator account, trading 1,000 shares each time. Because, really, who cares? It's all pretend money, right? After a few trades, they're either up like crazy or have completely bottomed out their pretend equity. And guess what? With a quick click, their account resets to $100,000 and they do it all over again.

To make the most of a simulator, you need to set it up to mimic how you're REALLY going to trade. If you plan to open a $10,000 trading account, set your simulator to $10,000 and treat it like you would a *real* $10,000 account.

Trade your plan—don't veer off into some crazy fantasy course that you'd never actually follow if this were real money.

When I first started trading, I would start my simulator at $50,000 and have at it. Sometimes I could trade and trade and trade, and sometimes I went bust in what felt like minutes. It didn't matter. It was just a simulator. When I ran out of "money," I just started over.

If that's all you want—to trade like it's a game—go for it. Blow up your fake trading account with ridiculous trades and move on.

But if you want to become a better trader—then take using the simulator seriously.

Plan the work and work the plan. Trade like you would if this were real money—YOUR real money.

Make mistakes and hone your strategy and see how things look in practice, not just in theory. **Once you "make money" consistently for 4 weeks in your simulator account, I suggest you start small with your "real money" account.** You'll hit the market ready to go, armed with the crucial, real markets-based know-how you've gained from your simulator work.

Done right, there's virtually no better tool out there.

MISTAKE #2: Trading with an Underfunded Account

Your account size should be geared to support the strategy and the markets you want to trade. If you're trading with an underfunded account, it usually makes you afraid to lose money and you're more likely to gamble.

Scratching your head? Let's break it down.

Hypothetically and just for illustrative purposes, let's say you open a $5,000 trading account, and you want to risk 2% on any given trade—that's a pretty good rule of thumb, universally. So, on your $5,000 account, you're willing to risk $100 on any given trade.

That might not sound like a lot, but think about it over the course of a day or a few days. If you lose $100 per trade over 10 trades, you're down $1,000 and your new trading account balance is $4,000. The good news? You can easily replace that $1,000. The reality? The difference between a $5,000 trading account and a $4,000 trading account isn't that significant in terms of the overall size of the account.

But let's say you have less in your account—$2,000, for example. If you're risking $100 per trade, you could easily slide down to $1,000 with 10 trade losses. That's half of your account—and that's hard to make back, especially if that hard hit damaged your confidence.

Let's go in the other direction—let's say you have $10,000 in your trading account and lose $1,000 on 10 trades, risking $100 on each trade. It's not ideal but, really, does it stop you in your tracks? Not so much. Your account balance is $9,000 and for most traders, that calls for a regroup and nothing more. Maybe you hit up the simulator and practice a bit but, hands down, you're going to press on and you're going to make that $1,000 back pretty quickly.

The common thread between these loss scenarios? *In each, you lost the same amount*—$1,000. But, depending on how well-funded your trading account was, it hit A LOT differently, didn't it? Losing $1,000 and having $9,000 left is A LOT different than losing $1,000 and having just $1,000 left.

When I first got to Austin, I started with $20,000 in my trading account. Within a few months, I'd lost $10,000. I freaked out—there's no nice way to put it. In my sheer hysteria, I started making mistakes and found myself terrified to execute a trade, even when I knew it was the right move. No doubt that hurt me more than it helped, both short-term and long-term.

While you don't need tens of thousands or hundreds of thousands of dollars to get started as a trader, you do need an adequately funded account.

An underfunded account is a ticking time bomb. Why?

Because YOU WILL LOSE MONEY at some point. If you can't afford to lose money—even in the name of MAKING money—then you're going to make bad decisions and you're going to wind up worse for the wear.

That *almost* happened to me. Then I course-corrected, got my legs back under me and powered forward. The rest, cliché as it sounds, is history. But I've seen just as many high-potential traders drop out completely, simply because they started with an underfunded account and couldn't handle the wear and tear that inevitably comes with this industry.

MISTAKE #3: Failing to EXECUTE Your Plan

To succeed in trading, you need a plan—and you need to act on that plan to make money. We went over this in detail in the last chapter.

If you don't act on your trading plan, it's the equivalent of reading diet books or watching exercise videos and expecting to lose weight without actually eating better and doing the exercises. In short, YOU WON'T. Until you act on the meal plans and workout routines, the scale's going to continue to creep up, up, up. Same goes for trading— except in trading, your account is going to creep down, down, down.

In a lot of ways, this one should go without saying. But as I've seen over and over, that's not the case. People THINK they want this lifestyle—the wealth, the financial freedom, the FREEDOM. And, I'd bet, they do deep down. But they're scared to break from the path they've always been on—the path that feels, but probably isn't, safer. So they develop a solid trading plan and do NOTHING.

You're reading this book because you want to plan your work and work your plan. You want to develop a rock-solid trading plan that tells you exactly what you're trading, at what times, what days and leveraging what methods.

A solid trading plan is the cornerstone of your trading business. Unfortunately many traders think that all they need is a trading strategy. This is NOT the case! Let me explain the difference between a trading strategy and a trading plan.

A trading strategy tells you when to enter and when to exit trades. A trading plan is more comprehensive than a tradingstrategy.

A trading plan covers at least seven elements:

- The market(s) you want to trade-stocks and options
- The timeframes you want to trade-60 min charts or daily charts.
- A brief description of the strategies you want to trade and when to use what strategy.
- The entry rules of the strategies.
- The exit rules of the strategies.
- Other important rules-when to trade and when not to trade.
- The money management approach you are using.

As you can see, a trading plan is a comprehensive document, but it doesn't have to be long. The best trading plan fits on one page, because simple is better at this stage!

And that's exactly what we're doing here with the PowerX Strategy and this book. By the time you hit the last page of the last chapter, you're going to be able to confidently say, "THIS is my plan—I'm going to trade every single night and, during the day, I'm going to spend 10 minutes checking the markets. I'm going to place trades according to the PowerX Strategy and use money management best practices. NO PROBLEM."

The reality? It should be NO PROBLEM. But, inevitably, many new traders fail. Why? Because they lack confidence and that lack of confidence in their trading plan or their ability to execute their trading plan can knock even the most focused, promising trader off track in an instant.

In order to become confident in your plan and your ability to execute the plan, it's important to make at least 40 trades in your simulator surrounding one particular strategy. If you want to trade the PowerX strategy, you need to place 40 trades on a simulator with the PowerX strategy. Not one. Not 10. Not 39. FORTY. 40 is the right number because it's large enough of a sample to be statistically relevant. We don't want to draw conclusions from too small a sample size. After you've completed 40 round-trip trades, then see where you land.

In addition, I suggest you are profitable in your simulator account for 4 weeks before trading your "real" money. Why 4 weeks? As you learn and make profits you'll most likely want to jump in too soon. After 4 weeks you'll have proven it long enough that it's more likely lasting. Also, 4 weeks is a better confidence booster than 2 weeks.

I know this might sound like a lot, but you MUST DO THIS. **This is how you prepare yourself for the market and pull yourself past all the wannabe traders out there.** Most traders look at the chart, think about what they already know about the PowerX Strategy and assume things will fall into place. But they have no numbers—they have nothing REAL backing it all up. They haven't placed those 40 simulator trades and proven they can be profitable for 4 weeks. And they, inevitably, suffer the consequences *big time.*

MISTAKE #4: UnRealistic Expectations.

This is a big one!

Recently somebody asked me: *"I have a $10,000 and I would like to make $20,000 within 3 months. Is this possible?"*

Everything is possible - after all, there are people who win millions in the lottery.

But it's not realistic.

In the previous chapter, we talked about realistic expectations: Trying to make $100 per week when you have a $10,000 account!

Unfortunately, many traders set their expectations way too high.

Let me give you an example:

When I was in high school, I was pretty tall. Therefore, my athletic coach asked me to do the high jump. I agreed, and we started training.

At first, he set the bar 2 feet high. I thought this was a joke. After all, I can WALK over a 2 feet high bar. I don't even have to jump.

But then my coach raised the bar: 2 inches at a time. Soon the bar was 3 feet high. Then 3½ feet. Then 4 feet. And before I knew it, the bar was 4½ feet high and I was struggling. I failed more often than I succeeded, and it was frustrating.

But that's what traders do: They set the bar too high in the beginning, because they don't know better, and then they get frustrated when they don't achieve their goals.

Recently I gave a talk in front of a room full of people. When I asked the room *"Do you think making $100 per week on a $10,000 account is realistic?"* - all hands went up. But there was this one gentlemen who said, *"It's too low!"* When I asked him what HE thought would be a realistic goal, he said *"I want to make at least $1,000 per week on a $10,000 account."* Based on my experience, he's setting himself up for failure.

Here's what happens if you set your goal too high: You will miss the goal more often than you achieve it. This will lead to frustration, and here's what a frustrated trader does: He buys a new trading system.

Don't make this mistake!

Set a small goal. Set the bar 2 feet high. Make sure you can realistically achieve this goal. Build your confidence. And when you achieve your goals <u>consistently</u>, start raising the bar. Set it to 2½ feet and see if you can still achieve this goal. If so, keep it there for a few weeks. Then you can raise your goal again. And if you struggle to make your goal, adjust the bar to a realistic level.

<u>Consistency is more important</u> than a high goal.

MISTAKE #5: Sweating the Small Stuff

Traders tend to worry about things that don't matter.

In my Live Trading Summits, I ask traders shortly after we start what they want to learn.

And it never fails:

There's ALWAYS an attendee who asks about how trading income will be taxed. Usually, it's a new trader starting with a $10,000 account.

And even though it is a valid question, it shouldn't be a big concern - YET.

Here's how the tax system works: You only get taxed on PROFITS that you make!

If you are new to trading, you should be worried about ONE THING and that's it. That one thing?

How to be PROFITABLE.

If you're overly worried about taxes, don't be. My rule of thumb? If your taxes exceed the value of your car, hire an accountant. If not, you're good. Take a breath.

At this point, you need to worry about trading and about being profitable as a trader.

Focus on making money first, THEN you can worry about how it is being taxed.

Once you start making money with trading, you can cross that bridge. And besides, I have people I work with that can help you with this.

The fact is, as your trading business grows, evolves and scales, things are going to change and you're going to have new decisions to make. But for now, don't get ahead of yourself. **Stay focused on the task at hand— becoming a profitable trader.**

Don't worry about things you can't control and bridges you've yet to cross. Focus on the task at hand. Focus on learning a profitable trading strategy and learning how you can make money trading.

Focus on making money first.

Because remember this: **When you can write a check for a solution to a problem, you don't have a problem!**

MISTAKE #6: Not Seeing the BIG PICTURE

That said, you DO need to see the big picture when you start trading. Just like I don't want you to worry about the endless WHAT IFS, I also don't want you getting so bogged down in a single trade that everything else starts to blur. Keep everything in perspective in every sense of the word.

A couple of losing trades shouldn't make a REAL impact on your overall progress as long as you have a solid plan. Now, YOU DO.

I see this happen a lot, though. I'll talk to a trader who did very well for months then experiences six losing trades in a row. It happens, and I, personally, would chalk it up to a bad day or week. We all have them and we always will.

Suddenly, though, this stellar trader is floundering, the wind completely knocked out of his sails. Even though his plan drove profits for him for MONTHS, he starts second-guessing everything. Six losing trades in a row, and now he's ready to change his plan—to completely gut it in favor of the untried and the untested?

My response? - No… just no!

This trader DOES NOT have to gut his system or reinvent his trading business. He needs to take a break, take a breath and move forward. He had six losing trades in a row. Until then he'd had winning streaks that put this negative experience to shame. He can't forget that. **This is where his trading journal is important.** He needs to check himself, preserve whatever momentum he can and keep going.

Always keep the big picture in mind.

MISTAKE #7: Being Afraid of Losses

Trading is a numbers game—and you need to know your numbers. That's why I suggest that you need to place at least 40 trades on a simulator before making any massive pivots—because you need to know your numbers backward and forward.

In that vein, you also need to understand losses and know what to expect—this 40-trade exercise will help you with that. Whether you're just starting out or have been trading for decades, understand that losses are a major part of this business.

You can't and won't make money without having losing trades!

Your job? Mitigate risk and keep your losses small.

You also have to keep your head in the game, which is impossible if you're obsessing about potential losses.

What we focus on expands. Focus on losses, and THAT'S what expands—and that's no good. You've heard this before, I'm sure. Someone shouts, *"Don't think about a pink elephant with red toe nails!"* Within a fraction of a second, the ONLY thing you can think about is a pink elephant with red toe nails. It's just the way our minds work.

The same concept applies to trading. If all you can imagine is that you're going to lose, YOU WILL. It will occupy your thoughts and dominate your days. That's the surest way to bottom out in this business.

Our brains do not understand the concept of the word "not."

So, when you say, *"I hope I don't get another loss,"* your brain hears *"I hope I get a loss"* and will do everything in its power to prove you right. And your brain will make sure that somehow "magically" you miss the winning trades and only take the losing trades. It never fails!

While I realize being positive day in and day out is easier said than done, you have to try. You have to keep your head-up and know you're in it to make money. And you need to psych yourself up, walking toward your computer with a decidedly "let's do this" attitude. Those are the traders who make money.

That's why I, personally, like the PowerX Strategy. It puts me in a better mindset because it is easy to use and proven, and when I'm in a better mindset, I make better trading decisions.

MISTAKE #8: Trading w/o Circuit Breakers

I'll say this one more time: *you need a stop-loss.* For EVERY single trade, you need to know your risk and you need to know how much you're *willing* to risk. When you're in this battle, the madness continues non-stop—it's you against the markets. This is an imperative part of your trading plan!

You need a daily risk limit, weekly limit, per trade limit, etc. You should also set a "catastrophic risk limit" on your account. That means that if you lose a preset amount—10%, 15%, 20%, let's say—you'll be automatically blocked from trading by your own account.

Again, these blocks aren't meant to deter you from trading or from the approach you're using. A string of losses happens to the best traders with the smartest and most strategically-sound systems. But, that said, there's no reason to send yourself into a losing freefall. We're trading, not gambling.

Mitigate risk. Know when to exit. Then take a breath, gather your thoughts and move on. This is the industry. This is the reality. It's better to embrace it now than let the losses drag you down and knock you out.

MISTAKE #9: IMPLODING

This happens when you don't have the right circuit breakers in place. Everything starts spinning out of control, and you have no systems in place to slow your descent. If you dodge mistake number eight you can, likely, dodge this one. But if you don't, you could easily find yourself in the implosion zone.

Here are a few scenarios:

Trading implosions tend to happen to traders in slow markets. You're waiting for opportunities and, still, nothing happens. So, you wait and wait and wait until that nagging little voice in your head chimes in and tells you, *"You have to TRADE to make money, pal. If you aren't trading, you aren't making money."*

You know your plan says to wait for the right opportunity which, some days, might not happen. Major reports get released. The Federal Reserve meets. Maybe even a holiday pops up midweek. But for some reason, the markets are quiet. And you start getting anxious.

You need to keep a broad perspective and not get bogged down in feeling like you MUST make a trade when there isn't meaningful opportunity. As a trader, you won't make money every single day. I don't—and I don't let it bother me.

But if you're underfunded, the market is slow, you feel this intense pressure to make a trade *and* you don't have circuit breakers keeping you in check, it's easy to roll toward total implosion.

Another way to implode? Trading without testing.

Here's the scenario: You've been observing things closely for some time and you're sure that just a few tweaks to the strategy you've been working successfully will produce even better results. So, you watch things even more closely and the next few trades *prove* that you're onto something. Naturally, you implement the tweaks into the next few trades and they work out as hoped.

NOW you're seriously READY to start trading THIS way—without running the 40 trade simulations. And that's a recipe for disaster, like I said before.

There's an old trading adage I've heard more times than I can count.

If a woman has a bad day, she buys a new pair of shoes.

If a trader has a bad day, they buy into a new system.

As a trader, you're most susceptible to the new—and the untried and untested—when you're in a slump. If you're making money with your approach it's largely due to the fact that you thoroughly tested your strategy over 40 trades and gained confidence in it as a result. Introducing new factors without testing them first is simply not the proper way to go and you know that already!

Keep this in mind: *The grass is always greener on the other side because it's fertilized with bullshit!*

So, chances are, you're staying the course and following the system you've been following because it had been working well to that point.

My advice? **In a slump, avoid distractions.**

You're too susceptible, and that's when bad decisions are made. Promise yourself you won't make any modifications to your strategy until you've proven over a sufficient number of trades that they'll actually improve results. When they do, you'll be in a better headspace and will be able to make smarter, more strategic and more meaningful decisions.

By the way, you're better off tracking that new strategy and trading it alongside your old strategy until it's clear that the new one is truly superior.

MISTAKE #10: Revenge Trading

There are certain people who crave revenge. When they feel they've been wronged, it occupies their thoughts around the clock.

I admit I've fallen into the "must get revenge" cycle more than a few times. I try not to—really, what does being vengeful ever accomplish? But sometimes, it's extremely hard. Sometimes, you've been burned and the only thing that will make you feel better is burning right back.

So, let's get this out of the way: you can't take revenge on the market. It just doesn't work that way.

The market is the market, and the market can easily humble even the best and most experienced of us.

Revenge trading? It just doesn't work. And, really, it doesn't make SENSE.

Keep THIS in mind:

- The market doesn't owe you.
- The market doesn't know if you've got a winning trade.
- The market doesn't know if you've got a losing trade.
- The market doesn't know if you're on a hot streak.
- The market can't—and won't—be pushed around. And it doesn't even realize you're trying to push it around.
- The market doesn't take revenge and you can't take revenge on the market.

Though this all sounds like a no-brainer, sometimes you'll need to remind yourself—because sometimes the sting is just that great. In short, don't revenge trade—or, more accurately, don't TRY to revenge trade. <u>The market doesn't care and the market won't ever bend to will.</u>

It's a waste of time, energy and resources to try. Just take a breath and move on. The market dictates what does and doesn't happen.

Follow your plan and keep making smart and strategic decisions as a result.

CHAPTER **8**

What it Takes to be a Trader

Everything up to this point feeds into a bigger topic: Do YOU have what it takes to be a trader?

I truly believe ANYONE can make money as a trader. It takes patience, focus and a desire to excel— really, a *trader's mindset.*

So, let's walk through a quick test I always give at my live events.

The goal? See who's the *perfect trader.* To play along, check the box next to all that apply to you, or print out the quiz at PowerXStrategy.com/gift

☐ *I am responsible for my own trading decisions.*

YOU are the one following the plan, you ALSO are the one who's responsible for sinking or swimming as a trader. If things aren't going your way, you are more than welcome to point a finger right at me and say, "Markus said THIS and Markus said THAT."

Go for it. At the end of the day, I'm responsible for my trading decisions and you're responsible for yours. I can give you the tools, resources and insights you need to be a successful trader. Whether or not you act on it is entirely up to you.

☐ *I understand losses are part of the business.*

In the previous chapter, we talked about how traders need to embrace the notion of loss—not every trade will be a win. And if it is? Call me. I want to see you in action, as do millions of other traders, academics and financial leaders.

I joke, but at the end of the day, I understand why this is so challenging. For our entire lives, we're judged on our ability NOT to make mistakes. The fewer mistakes we make on a test, the better the grade. The fewer mistakes we make in our jobs, the more successful we are. The fewer mistakes we make on the court, the field or the diamond, the better a player people believe we are—and the more our teams WIN.

Trading follows the same pattern. Just as with anything in life, there will be mistakes and losses. Reducing these and learning from them can be confusing and complicated. You need to understand that there is no "perfect game". The goal is to use a proven system that mitigates risk, reduces mistakes and losses and increases our profits. The sooner you can accept that you WILL have losses—the sooner you can move forward as a successful trader.

☐ *I accept that, early on, I won't be fully compensated for my time.*

I know, I know—you've invested time in reading this book and working through the PowerX Strategy and now you're ready to make money.

But you won't - not immediately, anyway.

Keep in mind,

There are FOUR STAGES of being a trader.
1. Losing money
2. Losing a little bit of money
3. Making a little bit of money
4. Making a lot of money

In the beginning, you'll likely be in the first two fields no matter how hard you try and how well you prepare. The better you prepare, though, the better the chances are that you'll make it as a trader in the not-too-distant future. But, in the beginning, you're not compensated for the time you put into building your trading business. Remind yourself it pays out LATER. Sometimes, you may have to remind yourself A LOT.

❏ *I understand that my plan is a work in progress.* Your plan will change—you'll learn from mistakes, you'll learn from your wins and you'll just LEARN. The easiest way to cut through the clutter and evolve your trading plan? **Write it all down**—the good, the bad, the ugly, the *really* ugly. This will prevent you from making the same mistakes over and over while reminding you of what's worked in the past. It takes seconds and, truly, can pay off with hundreds, thousands or even millions in incremental wins.

Some examples of what I've learned from my own trading past?

>I don't trade on Black Friday (the day after Thanksgiving).

>I don't trade when I'm sick.

>I don't trade when I'm preoccupied.

Recently, a renter in one of my investment properties texted me that their water heater wasn't working. I was distracted but tried to put it on the backburner until I was done trading. Guess what? I made stupid mistakes and lost a lot of money. And that's on me.

❏ *I review my trades daily, weekly and quarterly.* If you aren't doing it already, **KEEP A TRADING LOG**. Account statements are not enough!

The good news? If you don't have a trading log system, it's very simple and very straightforward. I'll even show you how in the next chapter.

❏ *I will never stop learning.*

Learn from every trade you make and from your trading log. See what's happening. See what's working and, equally importantly, what's NOT working. If you can crack the code on why, great. If not, then <u>focus your time and talent on doing MORE of what works and LESS of what doesn't</u>. It's as simple as that.

❏ *I own my plan.*

Every trader is different in terms of account size, available time to trade, risk preference and many other factors.

You have a plan and this is YOUR plan. This is not everyone else's plan. This is not MY plan. I own my OWN plan. I OWN Markus' trading plan. I don't own Jeff's trading plan or Jane's trading plan or Steve's trading plan. I own MY plan. You own YOUR plan. And that's all there is to it. Take ownership. Be proud and proactive. MAKE MONEY—and own those successes.

❏ *I am responsible for my own destiny.*

Whether you make it as a trader or not is your responsibility. You are reading this book and working through the PowerX Strategy because you want to learn—and you want to grow your long-term wealth. When you close this book, you're on your own. Will you sink or swim? Fly or fall? Drive wealth or get out of the way? It's up to you. <u>It's YOUR destiny.</u>

How many boxes did you check?

If you checked all of them, good for you: You have what it takes to be a trader.

If you couldn't check all of the statements above, read them again and let it sink in.

Because when trading, it's not only about the right trading strategy. The right mindset is even more important, because if your head is not in the right place, you'll make the wrong decision when it matters most.

CHAPTER 9

Know Your Numbers: The Importance of a Trading Log

Part of being a successful trader, is continuously monitoring your positions. While that might sound time-consuming, the reality is that it isn't—IF you're consistent in keeping a trading log.

You can't rely on account statements to tell the entire story. A simple Excel-based trading log will help you keep everything in check by putting the data front-and-center in a simple, easy-to-read and easy-to-digest format. **I'll even give you one that you can start with at PowerXStrategy.com/gift**

The only catch? A meaningful trading log relies on the TRADER. If you don't fill out your trading log consistently or don't input information you'll need or want down the road, your trading log is pretty much useless. That's not what you want.

Even a basic trading log will show you how profitable you are week over week, month over month, year over year and every time period in between. That's particularly helpful when you have a bad day or particularly down period.

A few bad losses can shake up even the best, most established trader. When that happens, you'll have your trading log to lean on, giving you some serious big-picture perspective that will help you stay on track—and on top of your approach.

Important Elements of a Trading Log

Your trading log should include a few key pieces of information:

- What is the stock symbol?
- When did you enter? When did you exit?
- What is the entry price? What is the exit price?
- Number of shares?
  - If using options, number of contract? Calls or puts?
- What market did you enter?
- What strategy did you use?
- Was it a profitable or a negative trade?
- Let's break down the specific elements of this example trading log. You can download this sample log at PowerXStrategy.com/gift

Trading Log for PowerX Strategy										
Entry Date	Symbol	Long/Short	Number of shares	Entry Price	Exit Date	Exit Price	Gross Profit/Loss	Comm.	Net Profit/Loss	Comments

COLUMN 1: ENTRY DATE

This is self-explanatory—this column shows WHEN you entered the trade once you are FILLED. It is best if you also enter the time of day you got filled in the trade.

COLUMN 2: SYMBOL

Are you trading TSLA? AMZN? AAPL? Include the symbol of the stock you placed the trade on.

COLUMN 3: LONG OR SHORT?

Did you buy or did you sell? If options, calls or puts?

COLUMN 4: NUMBER OF SHARES

How many shares or option contracts did you trade?

COLUMN 5: ENTRY PRICE

Here, log what PRICE you bought or sold at.

COLUMN 6: EXIT DATE

Simply enter when you exit the trade. This will help you to analyze how long on average you are staying in a trade. And you might discover important correlations between the duration of your trades and whether they are winners or losers. You can even add a column for "number of days" if you want. You will learn a lot from this stat.

For example, I have found that my "sweet spot" is to hold a trade for 3-20 days and that whenever I'm in a trade for longer than 20 days, it's usually a losing trade. Because of this, I simply added a rule to my plan that says, "Exit a trade after 20 days, even if neither the stop loss or profit target has been hit." THIS information is very powerful!

COLUMN 7: EXIT PRICE
In this column you will log the exit price of your trade.

COLUMN 8: GROSS PROFIT OR LOSS
After exiting the trade, note how much money you made or lost on this trade.

This is important to calculate important key performance indicators like Profit Factor, Average Winning Trade, Average Losing Trade, Average Profit Per Trade, etc.

COLUMN 9: COMMISSIONS
Enter how much you paid in commissions for this trade. This is important to analyze the impact of commissions on your trading.

COLUMN 10: NET PROFIT OR LOSS
Simply subtract the commission from your gross profit and loss and you will get the net profit and loss. If you want to track your percentage profit or loss, simply add a column for that.

COLUMN 11: COMMENTS

THIS is probably the most important field. After you exit the trade, take another look at the trade and write down what you learned.

Did you execute the trade according to your plan? Did you violate some rules? Did you make a mistake? THIS column will help you to quickly learn from your mistakes and make sure you're not repeating them. Because when it comes to trading, mistakes are usually costly.

You can take this a step further by adding columns for some of these specific questions you want to track. If you do this, you can simply enter "Yes" or "No" in the field so you can sort by them when you are analyzing your trades.

Maximizing the Comments Field

Here are a few more tips regarding the Comments field:

In this field I enter what happened during the trade. For example, *"short trade and a clean signal, which worked in my favor"*.

Or sometimes I'll indicate that I *"didn't like the trade, but took it anyhow"* which led to me making a mistake.

Put as much information in the comments as you possibly can.

When you're reviewing your trading logs weekly, having this information will help you gut-check, even if you've been away from the market or the particular trade for a few days.

As you're going through everything, you'll want to constantly ask yourself, *What could I be doing better? What do I need to improve on? What worked—and what didn't?*

Like I always say, **it's not about the goal, it's about the person you need to become in order to achieve the goal**. Your trading logs are a big piece of this.

What You'll Discover

When analyzing your trading logs, you might discover some interesting trends about your trading.

As an example, you might discover that you are making more money on your LONG trades than on your SHORT trades. So, what do you do? Focus on LONG trades only, and don't take any SHORT trades.

Or you might discover that trades that take longer than 20 days are typically losing trades. You might add a rule to exit a trade after 20 days.

You might discover that when you're trading stocks below $50, you lose money more often than on stocks that are priced above $50. If that's the case, add a rule to your trading plan that says, "Only trade stocks above $50."

Repeat this process over a few weeks or months and, inevitably, certain trends, shortcuts and preferences will bubble to the surface. Act on them, and don't stop tracking your trades.

This is, hands down, the simplest solution for improving your trades in a short period of time.

How to Store Your Trading Logs

Final note: be sure to store your trading logs *electronically*.

I had a student who would fax in trading logs—he would print them, fill them out by hand and fax them to me. Don't do that. <u>Keep your logs electronically so you always have them accessible and ready to be updated. This will also help you share them with mentors or coaches in the future.</u>

Regarding tools for creating a trading log, I suggest using an Excel Spreadsheet or a Google Spreadsheet because it's much easier to make some simple calculations and even sort the data for analyzing.

SPECIAL GIFT FOR YOU:

If developing your own trading log sounds overwhelming, we've provide one of our templates for you to download here: **PowerXStrategy.com/gift**

CHAPTER 10

Chart Your Own Course

I f you remember NOTHING ELSE from this book, remember this:

You don't have to be at the mercy of the Iceberg.

For every unsinkable ship—for every *Titanic*—there's an iceberg waiting in the distance to challenge its very core. For every seemingly endless market swing, there's a crash lurking around the corner. For every up, there's a down. For every win, there's a loss. For every epic achievement, there's an even more epic fail.

That's not meant to depress you—entirely the opposite. **Because the reality is, even during the slumps, the dips and the full-on disasters,** *people are making money.*

Not everyone. Not even a sizable chunk. But *some ARE* —and that will always be the case.

They're the people in speedboats zipping around the icebergs. They're the people who seem to be the exception to the rule. When the market's up, they're up. When the market's down, they're *still* up. It seems unfair. But, more so, it seems completely inevitable.

I want you to be one of *those people.* Stop envying and BE ENVIED. Stop worrying about the crash and learn to embrace and, even, harness its power. **Because the crash is coming. And, this time, *you can be ready* to not just get through it but to excel** *as a direct result of it.*

That starts here, with the stock and options trading process—the *PowerX Strategy* –outlined in this book. It continues every single day as you check your positions, make your entrances and exits and *take profits.*

I have one final piece of advice for you: consider finding a coach or a mentor. One of the biggest challenges to becoming a successful and consistent investor is second guessing yourself, especially if you have a bad day or week or if market conditions change. They can keep you in the game and make sure you're making smart strategic decisions. The right coach or mentor will hold you accountable, help you maintain perspective, and can guide you with their wisdom and experience.

If what you've read here makes sense to you and you are saying to yourself, "Yes! THIS is what I've been trying to understand about the markets. At last I get what I need to do to succeed!" then you may want to apply to work with our coaches at Rockwell Trading.

When choosing a coach, you need someone who explains the markets in a way you GET IT, has a history of helping diverse traders in diverse markets, will help you develop a trading plan and hold you accountable to stick with it!

When you are ready to shorten your learning curve and take your trading to the next level, you can go to PowerXStrategy.com/gift to apply for our coaching programs.

We'll hop on the phone with you and help you develop a custom trading plan for YOUR account size and trading needs. A plan that you will take with you even if you do not qualify to work with us at this time.

Coaching isn't for everyone.

It isn't for those looking for a get-rich-quick pill.

It isn't for those who think they are going to turn $10,000 into $1,000,000,000 in a year.

It isn't for those who are not ready to treat trading like a real business.

So who's it for?

Trading is for you if you are ready to live into the life you and your family deserve.

Trading is for you if you are ready to replace your income and finally quit your day job.

Trading is for those who have urgency to change your life right now!

Those with the commitment to follow through on a proven system.

Those who are coachable and ready to stand on the shoulders of those who came before you.

Those who are action takers and get out there an make life happen for them.

Those who are qualified financially and mentally to take their trading journey to the next level in the markets.

If this is you, then we can't wait to hear about your trading journey and evaluate together if Rockwell Trading will be a good fit to travel with you on your next leg to the freedom you desire.

Go to **PowerXStrategy.com/gift** to fill out the application and choose your time to meet with our coaches and we will help you create a custom trading plan for you as our gift to you.

THIS is how you'll drive wealth as a trader.

Study this information, practice it, and then execute. THIS is how you'll dodge the icebergs and the crashes *that happen and WILL happen* for the rest of your trading life. There are constant changes in the market but if you leverage the principles and processes of PowerX, it won't matter. Because you'll be primed to not just navigate the storm, but come out ON TOP—today and tomorrow.

Once again go to PowerXStrategy.com/gift to fill out the application and choose your time to meet with our coaches and we will help you create a custom trading plan for you as our gift to you.

We are here to support you into taking your next steps on your trading journey!

To Your Trading Success!

Markus Heitkoetter